Published under the auspices of
THE CENTER FOR JAPANESE AND KOREAN STUDIES
University of California, Berkeley

TALES OF TIMES NOW PAST

TALES OF TIMES

NOW PAST

Sixty-Two Stories
from a Medieval Japanese Collection

MARIAN URY

UNIVERSITY OF CALIFORNIA PRESS

BERKELEY • LOS ANGELES • LONDON

University of California Press
Berkeley and Los Angeles, California
University of California Press, Ltd.
London, England
©1979 by The Regents of the University of California
First Paperback Printing 1985
ISBN 0-520-05467-9
Library of Congress Catalog Card Number: 78-66019
Printed in the United States of America

1 2 3 4 5 6 7 8 9

for Edith Bloom and Hans Ury

Contents

Acknowledgments   xiii
Introduction   1
   A Note on Texts   22
Select Bibliography   24

KONJAKU MONOGATARI SHŪ

Tales of India

CHAPTER ONE
1 How Śākyamuni Tathāgata Came to Dwell
    in the World of Men   30
8 How Śākyamuni Preached the Dharma to Five Bhikshus   32
11 How the Buddha Entered a City of the Brahmans
    to Beg Food   33
18 How the Buddha Converted Nanda
    and Caused Him to Renounce Secular Life   35

CHAPTER TWO
1 About the Death of the Buddha's Father,
    King Śuddhodana   39
21 How a God Heard the Dharma
    and Obtained the Clear Vision of the Dharma Eye   40

CHAPTER THREE
14 About King Prasenajit's Daughter Ugly Adamantina   42
28 What the Buddha Said to the Sangha
    When He Was About to Enter Nirvana   44

CHAPTER FOUR
9 How Bodhidharma of India Went to This Place and That
    Observing the Devotions of the Monks   46
24 How Nāgārjuna, While a Layman,
    Made a Charm for Invisibility   49

34   How Two Brothers, Men of India,
     Carried Gold through the Mountains   51
41   How a Man for Love of His Child
     Went to King Yama's Palace   52

CHAPTER FIVE
2   How a King Went into the Mountains to Hunt Deer
     and Was Robbed of His Daughter by a Lion   54
13   How the Three Beasts Practiced the Way of the Bodhisattva
     and the Rabbit Roasted Himself   56

Tales of China

CHAPTER SIX
34   How a Novice of the K'ung-kuan Ssu in China
     Viewed the Lotus-Matrix World and Returned to Life   60
35   How Sun Hsüan-te Copied the Wreath Sutra   61

CHAPTER SEVEN
18   How a Nun of Ho-tung in China Chanted the Lotus Sutra
     and How the Text She Read from Was Altered   64

CHAPTER NINE
4   How Someone in Lu-chou Killed a Neighbor
     and Was Not Punished   66
44   How Mo Yeh of China Made a Sword
     and Presented It to the King
     and How His Son, Broad-of-Brow, Was Killed   67
45   How Hou Ku Tricked His Father
     and Prevented an Unfilial Act   70

CHAPTER TEN
1   How Shih-huang of Ch'in Governed
     from His Palace at Hsien-yang   71
8   How Wu Chao-hsiao of China Saw a Poem on the Water
     and Loved Its Author   76
12   How Chuang Tzu Went to Someone's House
     and How His Host Killed a Goose to Serve with the Wine 78
13   How Chuang Tzu Observed the Behavior
     of Dumb Creatures and Fled   79

Tales of Buddhism in Japan

CHAPTER ELEVEN

3   How E no Ubasoku Recited Spells
    and Employed Demonic Deities   82
4   How the Venerable Dōshō Went to China,
    Was Transmitted the Hossō Teachings,
    and Returned Home   84

CHAPTER TWELVE

28 How a Government Clerk of Higo Province
    Escaped a Rakshasa   87

CHAPTER THIRTEEN

10 How the Sutra Chanter Shunchō
    Exhibited the Lotus Sutra's Efficacy   90
39 About Two Men in Izumo Province,
    Reciters of the Wreath and Lotus Sutras   92

CHAPTER FOURTEEN

3   How a Monk of the Dōjōji in the Province of Kii
    Copied the Lotus Sutra and Brought Salvation to Serpents 93
5   About a Man Who Copied the Lotus Sutra
    to Save the Soul of a Fox   96

CHAPTER FIFTEEN

28 How a Priest of Chinzei Who Ate Carrion
    Was Reborn in Paradise   99

CHAPTER SIXTEEN

17 How Kaya no Yoshifuji, of Bitchū Province,
    Became the Husband of a Fox and Was Saved by Kannon 102
20 How Travelers from Chinzei, Through Kannon's Aid,
    Escaped Being Killed by Bandits   105
32 How an Invisible Man Regained Corporeal Form
    through Kannon's Aid   110

CHAPTER SEVENTEEN

1   About a Monk Who Prayed to Meet a Manifestation
    of the Bodhisattva Jizō   114

2   How Ki no Mochikata Worshipped Jizō
     and Benefited from His Favor   115
44 How a Monk through Bishamonten's Aid Begot Gold
     and Obtained a Means of Support   117

CHAPTER NINETEEN
8   How a Falconer in the Western Part of the Capital
     Renounced Secular Life Because of a Dream   121
24 About the Monk Whose Name Was Entered on a Petition
     to the God of Mount T'ai to Take the Place of His Master 124

CHAPTER TWENTY
35 How Shinkai, a Monk of Mount Hiei, Suffered Retribution
     in This Present Life for Jealousy   127

                    Secular Tales of Japan

CHAPTER TWENTY-TWO
8   How Great Minister Tokihira
     Got Major Counselor Kunitsune's Wife   134

CHAPTER TWENTY-THREE
14 How Taira no Munetsune, Lieutenant of the Left Division
     of the Outer Palace Guards, Escorted High Priest Myōson 139

CHAPTER TWENTY-FOUR
2   How Prince Kaya Made a Doll
     and Set It Up in the Ricefields   142
23 How Minamoto no Hiromasa Ason
     Went to the Blind Man's House at Ōsaka   143
24 How the Lute Genjō Was Snatched by an Oni   146

CHAPTER TWENTY-FIVE
11 How Fujiwara no Chikataka's Son Was Taken Hostage
     by a Robber and Freed through Yorinobu's Persuasion   150

CHAPTER TWENTY-SIX
9   How Men of Kaga Province Who Went to an Island
     Where a Snake Was Warring with a Centipede
     Aided the Snake and Settled in the Island   153

CHAPTER TWENTY-SEVEN

15 How a Woman Who Was Bearing a Child
Went to South Yamashina, Encountered an Oni,
and Escaped   161

22 How the Hunters' Mother Became an Oni
and Tried to Devour Her Children   163

29 About the Two Wet-Nurses
in the House of Middle Captain Masamichi
Who Looked Exactly Alike   165

41 How the Fox of Kōyagawa Turned into a Woman
and Rode on Horses' Croups   167

CHAPTER TWENTY-EIGHT

5   How Tamemori, the Governor of Echizen,
Subdued the Junior Officers
of the Six Companies of the Guards   172

11 How Kaishu, the Intendant of Gion,
Was Given as a Fee for Chanting the Sutras   177

38 How Fujiwara no Nobutada, Governor of Shinano,
Took a Tumble at Misaka   179

CHAPTER TWENTY-NINE

18 How a Thief Climbed to the Upper Story of Rashō Gate
and Saw a Corpse   183

23 How a Man Who Was Accompanying His Wife
to Tanba Province Got Trussed Up at Ōeyama   184

28 How a Beggar Who Lived in the Area South of Kiyomizu
Used a Woman to Lure Men into His House
and Killed Them   186

CHAPTER THIRTY

5   How a Poor Man Left His Wife,
and How She Became the Wife of the Governor of Settsu 192

CHAPTER THIRTY-ONE

7   How the Minor Controller of the Right Moroie no Ason
Encountered a Woman and Died   195

31 About the Old Woman Who Sold Fish
at the Headquarters of the Crown Prince's Guard   197

37 About the Great Oak in Kurumoto District
in Ōmi Province   199

Acknowledgments

This translation had its beginning in a suggestion made by Douglas E. Mills; my debt to Dr. Mills is truly *kagiri nashi* (to borrow a favorite phrase of the *Konjaku* compiler's) and it is a pleasure to be able to acknowledge it here. Others to whom I am greatly obliged are Zelda Bradburd and Bonnie Crown, whose faith in the book helped make it reality; Benjamin Wallacker, Joanne Lafler, and Dan McLeod, who showed exemplary patience in reading portions of the draft and made helpful suggestions; and Everett Jameson, a distinguished authority on Japanese falconry, whom it was my special good fortune to be able to consult. I am grateful also to Dr. Kawaguchi Hisao, who generously took time from a busy schedule to answer a crucial query; and, of course, to Donald Shively for many, many acts of practical kindness. I have had much profit from discussions with W. Michael Kelsey, and I would be negligent if I failed to thank him for letting me read in draft the critical portion of his "Didactics in Art: The Literary Structure of *Konjaku Monogatari-shū*" (Ph.D. dissertation, Indiana University, 1976), containing an analysis and complete translation of Chapter Nineteen. My work in its initial stages was supported in part by a University of California Regents' Summer Faculty Fellowship. I wish there were someone I might thank for aid in preparing the manuscript; but I typed it myself. Gladys Castor was my kind and perspicacious editor.

Introduction

Konjaku monogatari shū, the work from which these stories come, is a collection of over a thousand brief tales from medieval Japan. *Monogatari,* literally "a telling," is a word for tales or narratives of any kind; *shū* means collection or anthology; *konjaku* is the Sino-Japanese pronunciation for the two Chinese characters in the formulaic phrase with which each tale opens. (The phrase itself, read in Japanese, is *ima wa mukashi,* in my translation "at a time now past.") The collection is encyclopedic in scope and arrangement. We do not know exactly when it was compiled, although 1120 seems a not unlikely approximate date for its completion—if indeed it was quite completed. We do not know who the compiler was, or even whether he was one or many. If one, he was almost certainly not Minamoto Takakuni, to whom tradition ascribes the work, if only because Takakuni died in 1077. Takakuni was a devout Buddhist; the compiler may well have been a Buddhist lay-monk, someone who would have entered religion comparatively late in life at the end of a secular career. The compiler was almost certainly a monk of some sort, perhaps an archivist or the like, in one of the monastic establishments on Mount Hiei, the great center of the Tendai sect of Buddhism and thus of Japanese Buddhism in general during the Heian period (794–1185). Takakuni was an aristocrat; the compiler's origins, however, were probably somewhat humbler. And furthermore, it can easily be demonstrated that *Konjaku* could not be the work of just one man, for no single individual could have had the energy to execute unaided so vast and varied a work; nor is it likely that the skilled storyteller who recorded the best and most complex of the stories could be the literal-minded drudge who recorded many of the others. But then, it can with equal ease be demonstrated that *Konjaku* could only be the work of one man: only one man could have been so consistent in the use of narrative formulas, in the preference (a modern one) for showing over telling, dramatic presentation over explanation. Only one man, moreover, could have ordered the individual stories within the chapters so consistently and so minutely. Perhaps there was a

committee of redactors headed by some forceful individual —
although again, this explanation seems not quite satisfactory. But
whoever and however many they were, there is obviously a con-
trolling intelligence at work, which for the sake of convenience
throughout this book I shall refer to as the "*Konjaku* compiler."
Whoever this hypothetical compiler was, he was a man of a
lively, ironical, and pragmatic turn of mind, with an eye for the
absurd and for the telling detail. He had a keen interest in the
supernatural, especially its unpleasanter manifestations, and
gave practical advice on how to deal with it. Living a century later
than Lady Murasaki, the author of the *Tale of Genji,* in a different
milieu, he was not unaware of those finer feelings her romance
celebrates; if he did not, one suspects, experience them himself,
he nevertheless appreciated them as part of the curious human
scene. All bonds of love, he wrote, come from karma. For the most
part, though, he counseled men to beware, for the promise of a
love adventure was all too apt to lure you into a den of brigands —
if not worse. He had a broad but often sketchy education. He
lacked the aristocratic love of poetry, although he could appreci-
ate the composition of a poem as a virtuoso feat, comparable to
those performed by carpenters, painters, musicians, and Taoist
diviners. His interest in the secular world was as vigorous as his
piety.

The precise purpose for which the compilation was made is
also rather a mystery, and perhaps if we knew it we would have
better answers to the other questions about it. There is no preface.
It has been suggested that the compiler may have worked simply
for his own amusement; and it is true that what might be called a
magpie tendency can be found throughout much of premodern
Japanese literature. It is probable, however, that the motive was
religious and that behind the compilation was a very practical
intention: to provide a handbook of stories which preachers
might use to enliven their sermons. But then, a third of the
chapters are composed of stories on secular subjects. Perhaps they
are there because the book burst the bounds of its original plan; or
because secular stories could also be used by the preacher, to draw
a crowd. The compiler's stance, in any event, is determinedly
didactic, and no doubt he felt that good advice is good advice,
whether it has to do with accumulating good karma, or how to get
on in the world (which may amount to the same thing), or how to

keep from looking ridiculous, or keep from being cheated when you buy food. The stories comprehend the whole of life as the compiler envisioned it, representing all three countries of the known world, all the provinces of Japan, and the activities of persons of every class of society.

The use of a handbook is easier if it is systematically arranged. *Konjaku* was designed to be in thirty-one *maki* (a division which may be translated "books" but which I shall translate "chapters"). This is their order:

CHAPTERS ONE TO FIVE: Tales of India, beginning with the founding of Buddhism.

One. The birth, enlightenment, and ministry of Śākyamuni, the historical Buddha.

Two. The deaths of the Buddha's parents; parables and other stories in which the Buddha teaches the workings of karma.

Three. More stories of the Buddha's ministry, involving every class of believer. The chapter closes with the Buddha's nirvana.

Four. Stories about the Buddha's disciples after his death; miracle tales of the "three jewels" of Buddhism.

Five. Jataka tales, which take place before the Buddha's birth; miscellaneous tales about India.

CHAPTERS SIX TO TEN: Tales of China, beginning with the establishment of Buddhism.

Six. The transmission of Buddhism to China; its propagation; miracle tales about the Buddha's images.

Seven. Miracle tales about the sutras, especially the Mahāprajñāpāramitā and the Lotus (Saddharmapuṇḍarīka) sutras.

Eight. [This chapter is missing. It is thought that it was intended to contain more miracle tales.]

Nine. Secular tales teaching filial piety; tales of visits to hell; Buddhist tales teaching the principle of karma.

Ten. Secular history, beginning with the founding of the Chinese empire; biographical anecdotes and romance.

CHAPTERS ELEVEN TO TWENTY: Tales of Buddhism in Japan.

Eleven. The transmission of Buddhism to Japan; its propagation; tales about the establishment of the great temples.

Twelve. Tales about the establishment of Buddhist ceremonies and festivals; miracle tales about the various Buddhas and the Lotus Sutra.

Thirteen. Tales illustrating the merit to be acquired by reciting the Lotus Sutra.

Fourteen. More miracle tales, of the Lotus and other sutras.

Fifteen. Stories of men and women reborn in Amida's paradise.

Sixteen. Miracles of Kannon.

Seventeen. Miracles of various other bodhisattvas, chiefly Jizō.

Eighteen. [Missing. It has been suggested that this chapter was to have been modeled on the two preceding ones.]

Nineteen. Tales of religious conversion; strange tales illustrating the principle of karma.

Twenty. A few tales of a kind of goblin called *tengu;* tales of visits to hell; tales of karmic retribution in this present life.

CHAPTERS TWENTY-ONE TO THIRTY: Secular tales of Japan.

Twenty-one. [Missing. It is thought that this chapter was to have provided an anecdotal history of the imperial house.]

Twenty-two. Anecdotes about the Fujiwara family (hereditary regents and prime ministers), from its founding.

Twenty-three. Anecdotes about feats of strength and daring.

Twenty-four. Anecdotes about masters of the sciences (e.g., medicine), crafts, and arts.

Twenty-five. Tales about warriors.

Twenty-six. Popular tales the events of which are explained through karma.

Twenty-seven. Tales of malevolent supernatural creatures.

Twenty-eight. Humorous stories.

Twenty-nine. Tales of robbery and violence; tales about animals.

Thirty. "Poem-tales" (tales derived from those of an older type, in which the central event is the creation or exchange of poems).

Thirty-one. Strange tales from the provinces.[1]

Some of the chapters (e.g., 22) are not fully extant; some must never have been completed.

The corpus of material available to the anthologist was of a different kind for each country; India, especially, was different because it was known by the Japanese only through religion. But granted this, it is obvious that the compiler has, at the very least, arranged the tales of each country so as to describe the same general movement. In each case the collection progresses from founders to followers; from major founders to lesser founders; from the sacred to the secular; from the highly edifying to the merely instructive. Much more precise symmetries have been discerned by painstaking scholars. It requires only a little effort to see in the fourth and fifth chapters, dealing with India, a parallel to the ninth and tenth chapters, dealing with China, and to the twenty-first through thirty-first chapters, dealing with Japan. The Japanese scholar who has devoted the most attention to the structure of *Konjaku* is Kunisaki Fumimaro, and one of his observations is that the chapters of secular tales of Japan in turn reiterate the Buddhist ones in overall arrangement, falling into three parts: history (the missing chapter 21, paralleling chapter 11 and the first ten stories in chapter 12); praise of persons (chapters 22–25, paralleling the remainder of chapter 12 and chapters 13–18, praise of Buddhism); and instruction (chapters 26–31, paralleling chapters 19–20). He suggests also that, at the same time, chapters in this final section are constructed to form pairs; for example,

1. These descriptions of the contents of the chapters are adapted rather freely from those appearing in Mabuchi, I, 32–35. (For complete citations of books and articles cited in brief in the notes, see the Select Bibliography.) A similar list, with slightly different emphases, may be found in Mills, *A Collection of Tales from Uji*, pp. 24–25. There is a strong relationship between *Uji shūi monogatari* and *Konjaku monogatari shū*, although its precise nature is highly problematical; Mills summarizes and discusses the significant modern Japanese scholarship on the origin of both texts, making some additional suggestions on the basis of his own research. Readers in search of detailed information about the controversies surrounding the very difficult question of the origin and authorship of *Konjaku* are referred to his painstaking study.

Chapters Twenty-two and Twenty-three illustrate two kinds of strength, political and physical, while the arts and skills of the city-bred in Chapter Twenty-four have their counterpart in those of provincial warriors, in Chapter Twenty-five.[2]

Within each chapter the stories are meticulously arranged. As a rule, they appear in pairs joined by a common theme; in addition, each member of the pair will have associations with the other story adjacent to it through some common motif. (Associative linking as a literary technique is well known to scholars of Japanese poetry,[3] although in general it might be wrong to make too much of the resemblance.) For example, in Chapter Twenty-eight, a story about a man who is afraid of cats owing to an enmity in a previous life (story 31) is followed by a story of a man who is afraid of snakes for the same reason (story 32). This pair in turn is followed by one in which the common element is outrageous behavior by servants: in the first, someone's attendant kisses a tortoise and is bitten (story 33); in the second, a soldier unthinkingly spits in his master's dish and, despite his valor, gets a reputation as a fool (story 34). The link between the two pairs is the two creatures, snake and tortoise.

There are instances in which recurrent themes are used throughout an extended sequence (and here the resemblance to the poetry anthology is more marked). Such a sequence (also in chapter 28) begins with two stories involving poisonous mushrooms: in the first, a poor monk eats them in the hope of enjoying nice funeral gifts (story 17); this is followed by its mirror image, the story of a wealthy monk whose impatient disciple tries to poison him with mushrooms only to be told that the master has been making a steady diet of them for years (story 18). The mushroom motif disappears a few stories later, and then reappears in a story of nuns who go into the mountains, eat mushrooms, and begin to dance (story 28). The link between that story and the one immediately preceding it is dancing: an official betrays his humble past as a traveling entertainer when, upon hearing music, he

2. Kunisaki Fumimaro, "*Konjaku monogatari* no setsuwa to soshiki no dokujisei," in Kanda Hideo and Kunisaki Fumimaro, eds., *Nihon no setsuwa*, vol. 2 (Tokyo: Tōkyō bijutsu, 1974), pp. 240–262. A detailed exposition of Kunisaki's major ideas about the structure of the work as a whole appears in Frank, *Histoires*, pp. 16–26.

3. See Robert H. Brower and Earl Miner, *Japanese Court Poetry* (Stanford: Stanford University Press, 1961), esp. pp. 319–329.

starts dancing (story 27). In between these two pairs there arise and mingle contrapuntally such motifs as diet in general, embarrassing revelations, eccentric personal appearance and habits, and nicknames.

Stories that are known to have originated at a time later than Takakuni's are part of such closely integrated sequences, and this is a good reason for denying that the book could have been essentially completed by Takakuni, to be supplemented here and there by some later hand. The need to fill out sequences, moreover, is one possible explanation for the presence of dull and inferior stories along with the superior ones. Internal ordering so minute goes far beyond the demands of indexing. And the placing of a particular story in one chapter rather than another often seems determined by the need to form a particular sequence rather than by the most conspicuous aspect of its subject matter. The story "How Men of Kaga Province Who Went to an Island Where a Snake Was Warring with a Centipede Aided the Snake and Settled in the Island" (26:9, or chapter 26, story 9) might as easily have been put in Chapter Twenty-seven, for example, since it deals with supernatural creatures; the concluding remark that it was their karma that caused the men to go to the island and settle there is an obvious addition to a traditional story about origins. But the story was needed to form a pair with another, which is about the settlement of an island but does *not* involve supernatural beings (26:10).[4] With so many possibilities, a story might easily appear in duplicate, had the compiler been inattentive — but there are no instances of inclusion of the same story in two different chapters.

The compiler's care for arrangement is symptomatic of his ambitiousness. The surviving manuscripts show some damage from insects; nevertheless it is likely that the reason three chapters are lacking in their entirety and others are lacking in part is not that, once written, they were lost, but that they could never be written at all. Emperors, the subject of Chapter Twenty-one, can be a ticklish subject; and it is thought that the compiler must have expected that material to form Chapters Eight and Eighteen would be abundant and had then been disappointed. His ambi-

---

4. The story in question is of the founding of Imosejima, "brother-and-sister island"; a close parallel appears in *Uji shūi monogatari* and is translated by Mills, pp. 222–223.

tions for his book proved, in the end, to be larger than his ability
to realize them.

The concern for order and pattern that can be seen in the
arrangement of the chapters and the stories within them appears
in the telling of the individual stories as well. Each begins with
the same formula. (The exact meaning of *ima wa mukashi* is still
a subject of debate among scholars, and I have chosen rather
arbitrarily among their interpretations in translating; what is
most important is just that it is a formula.) The formula is almost
always followed by a stereotyped introduction of the protagonist
(if a servant, sometimes of his master). It is worth remarking that
this introduction is repeated with each new story even when the
same protagonist appears in adjacent stories: the compiler was
very conscious that his aim was to record individual stories, not to
produce a naive version of narrative history or biography. Within
the story there are frequent repetitions of such phrases as *sono
toki ni*, "just at that time," *sono nochi*, "after that," *shikaru aida*,
"now, however." The phrases help make the telling explicit; the
style contrasts with the flowing, allusive language of the court
romances of the age. Such expressions underscore the rhythm of
the events and provide breathing spaces.

The narration itself gives a prominent place to conversations;
events which in tellings of the same story elsewhere are only
described are in *Konjaku* made into conversations. The stories are
often blocked off into scenes, as a play might be: the compiler has
a special love of scenes in which everything freezes, as in the
kabuki drama of a later era,[5] and, among these, especially scenes
in which spectators stare open-mouthed or in which people are
waiting expectantly for something that isn't going to happen
(19:24, 28:11). Often the end of a scene is signaled with the word
kaerinu, literally "he/they returned home." It has been suggested that if *Konjaku* was indeed a handbook for preachers, the
telling of the story to an audience might have been accompanied
by a display of pictures. Presentation of that sort would indeed
have been best served by a style of narration that exploits the
dramatic possibilities of individual scenes.

Each story ends with a moral; where no moral seems to have

5. I am indebted to Professor Robert Brower for this observation.

come easily to mind, there may be a comment in the form of a moral: that the story has been attested to, that this is a queer happening, that the world is really like that. Sometimes this "moral" asks for an explanation. How could a man eat poisonous mushrooms and not die? Why is it that a man who was tricked by a fox on the first encounter was not tricked on the second? As often with the Aesopic fable, the moral sometimes applies to only a part of the story, or is not equal to the complexity of what the story itself teaches, or is one — and not the most obvious — of many possible morals.[6] That the moral *be there* is at least as important as what it says: neither the compiler's formal drive nor his didactic urge will allow him quite to relinquish the opportunity. Each story closes with a formulaic phrase, almost always *to namu katari-tsutaetaru to ya*. The phrase emphasizes the fact that the story is secondhand.

Konjaku monogatari shū belongs to a large and miscellaneous genre of collections of narrative that modern Japanese literary historians call *setsuwa bungaku*, tale literature. One of the characteristics of these works is that they were not thought of by their authors as literature — although when someone has put himself to as much trouble as has the compiler of *Konjaku* one is inclined to wonder. This genre, which flourished in the Heian and Kamakura periods (794–1333), includes small as well as large collections of tales, collections that are explicitly devoted to sacred subjects as well as those, like *Konjaku*, of mixed content, and some also essentially of secular content. A subgenre is that of the *ōjōden*: collections of biographies, *den*, of persons who have achieved *ōjō*, rebirth in paradise. In some collections the contents are systematically ordered; in some they are not. None is ordered quite like *Konjaku*. In some, the stories are written in Chinese (in premodern Japan the ordinary written language of educated men); in some, they are in Japanese (the medium for poetry and romance); in some, they are in Japanese influenced in varying degrees by Chinese usage and vocabulary. *Konjaku* falls into the last of these categories; it is written in a special orthographic style

6. For example, in many early collections of Aesop's fables, the moral of the story about the fox and the grapes is not the familiar one about self-delusion but rather praises the wisdom of the fox for learning to be content with what he has.

called *senmyō-gaki,* a popular medium at that time among clerks and clerics. Whether Chinese or Japanese or some mixture, the language of *setsuwa* is usually unornamented, but this again is not an invariable rule. What the collections have in common is that the stories they contain are secondhand; are presented as true, or at least as *possibly* true; and are short.

The word *setsuwa* may be translated "tales" if it is kept in mind that they are tales of a particular sort. Or, depending on what aspects of the tales one has in view, the word may be translated "legend" or "anecdote." In form, they are anecdotes. Anecdote may be defined as the narration of an individual event, or a series of events. It is sometimes said that anecdote does not concern itself with character, but this, I think, is wrong. Its subject is in fact character — as delineated by the event. And the character need not be of an individual man only; it can be that of a class of men, a situation, a dilemma, or a world. John Aubrey's *Brief Lives* is an attempt to delineate its author's world through anecdote. The anecdote sees its subject in terms of observable action. Significantly, the *ōjōden,* as has been pointed out, pay little attention to their protagonists' state of mind or even their holy life; what interested the authors was the specific event of the rebirth in paradise: the deathbed portents and the reactions of the witnesses.[7]

The anecdote proceeds from the conviction that there is something remarkable about its subject. At its best it is both typical and astonishing. "Yes, that's the sort of thing he *would* do," the reader should think to himself. "That's the sort of thing persons of that sort *would* do." "That is the sort of thing that is always happening to people who get themselves into that kind of fix." But at the same time, "I would never have guessed he was capable of quite that!" "Fancy such things existing!" The best anecdotes, revealing aspects of their subject that would otherwise have remained hidden, extend our knowledge. Massed together, they can form portraits which are complex and comprehensive. Boswell's *Life of Johnson* is anecdote depicting a man; *Konjaku monogatari shū* is anecdote depicting a world.

The English word "legend" has two senses, both of which are

---

7. Ikegami Jun'ichi, *"Konjaku monogatari shū* no hōhō," in Kanda Hideo and Kunisaki Fumimaro, eds., *Nihon no setsuwa,* vol. 2, pp. 263–292.

appropriate to *Konjaku*. *Setsuwa* are legends in the sense of the German word *Sagen*, that is the counterpart in folklore of written history (as opposed to *Märchen*, the counterpart of written fiction). Those in the first twenty chapters of *Konjaku* are also legends in the sense of the German *Legende*, the pious tale, such as in the West appears in the *Legenda Aurea* of Jacobus de Voragine, intended to be read and read aloud. Not all *setsuwa* in all collections are didactic, but when they are, the way in which they teach is related to the fact that they were meant to be true accounts of events. *Konjaku* has the practicality of its wisdom in common with Aesop; but unlike Aesop or the medieval *Gesta Romanorum*, which has sometimes been suggested as the Western counterpart to *Konjaku*, it does not teach by allegory. Its method is example; the compiler shows us how someone has behaved and whether the result of his behavior was reward or misfortune, and bids the reader take heed. The compiler is giving information about the real world, and his intended reader's belief is an essential ingredient in this process. The reader need not believe fully — but he has a commitment to try. (This is true even where the story is improbable — perhaps especially where the story is improbable. The task for the purveyor of marvels is to strain the reader's credulity without breaking it.) Stories that are obviously fiction lack this sort of monitory value. The point is worth making because it bears on the way that *setsuwa* function as literature. A number of the stories in *Konjaku* work very well when we read them as we read fiction: an example might be the story of a young couple who escape from bandits (16:20); but for the original readers it would surely have added to the excitement to know that this could happen to you too if you traveled in remote places. Even such a story as that of the fish-vendor who is discovered to be selling snake meat (31:31) can be read in the modern way: though there is no attempt by the compiler to elicit sympathy for the old woman, *we* are likely to engage in musings on the social conditions that induced her to engage in such repellent trickery, and we may be struck, as was the essayist and short-story writer Akutagawa Ryūnosuke, by the starkness and brute vigor of the scene. But, strictly speaking, a story that chiefly relates that a crone has been selling tainted food — or that a holy man has cultivated meritorious karma through some odd religious practice — is not of interest if it is known to be fiction; it is of interest if it is telling us something we did not know about the world, and it is especially so if it is telling us something we would scarcely have suspected without it.

That things are often not what they seem is one of the compiler's fundamental assumptions; it is no accident that one of the most common narrative modes in *Konjaku* is that of discovery (something that it has in common, rather improbably, with the fiction of Henry James). A beautiful woman is discovered to be a murderer's decoy (29:28) or a fox (14:5); a venerable grandam is discovered to be one of that tribe of ogres the Japanese call *oni* (27:15, 27:22); a provincial governor is discovered to be even more venal than his subordinates had suspected (28:38). This is the attitude of the ironist; but it is important, also, to note that Buddhism conceives of the process of enlightenment as one in which appearances are discovered to be false. The saint and devotee are more percipient than ordinary men. By such persons apparent wastrels and eccentrics are discovered to be holy monks (4:9), an outcaste with filthy habits to be pure at heart (15:28), an abused child to be the Bodhisattva Jizō (17:1).

The people in the stories are real people, not fictional characters. Some are otherwise unknown and are met with only once; but such persons as the diviner Abe no Seimei (19:24) and the great lover Taira no Sadabumi (22:8) can also be found in the history books and appear in many other *setsuwa*.

Since *Konjaku* concerns itself with the real world, it follows that it depicts the things of the world in concrete and detailed terms. This is true even of the first ten chapters, where the compiler ordinarily deviates very little from his textual sources. He pauses in the story of a man who uses a charm for invisibility to record the means of its manufacture (4:24). Akutagawa, who was chiefly responsible for the twentieth century's discovery of *Konjaku* as literature, remarked with delight on the vividness of a brief passage in the tale of the three beasts that seek food for an elderly beggar who is a god in disguise (5:13). Nothing corresponding appears in the story's source, in the *Ta-t'ang hsi-yü chi*, and it was therefore most likely the compiler's own addition: "...the rabbit... pricked his ears up and arched his back, widened his eyes and flexed his forelegs and opened the gap in his hindquarters, scampering. ...."

This taste for the concrete extends to names of persons, reigns, ranks, offices, villages, temples. Typically, when the spirit of a monk named Kyōshin appears to someone on earth to report that he has been reborn in paradise, he not only identifies himself but gives his exact address (15:26, not translated). In a few stories the protagonist is identified merely as "a man," "a woman," "a person of humble birth"; there are a few also in which the compiler says, "I don't know who he was exactly, but. . . ." Whenever possible, however, he supplies precise information. Sometimes it must not have been possible, and then there is a space in the text, which the compiler no doubt intended to fill in when he had acquired the requisite information. There are a great many of these lacunae; and that is another reason for thinking that *Konjaku* was both uncompleted and uncompletable.

The sources of *Konjaku's* legends are various. For the tales of India they are generally the sacred books of Buddhism, which contain a wealth of stories from Indian oral tradition. The Japanese knew these, of course, in their Chinese translations. For the tales of China, the sources are histories, didactic works such as the Classic of Filial Piety, and a rich literature of collections of "strange tales." One such collection, compiled during the T'ang in the service of Buddhism, was the *Ming-pao chi*, which furnished a large proportion of the tales in Chapters Seven and Nine of *Konjaku*.[8] For the religious chapters of the Japanese section the sources are, by and large, earlier collections of *setsuwa*, including the *Nihon ryōiki* (ca. 822?), the earliest work in the genre, itself inspired in part by the *Ming-pao chi*. Others included the *ōjōden* and such works as *Dai Nihon Hokke genki* (1041)[9] and *Jizō*

---

8. By informed count, 49 of the 174 tales in all the extant Chinese section of *Konjaku* come from the *Ming-pao chi*; the total number of tales in the text of the latter that has been shown to be the one used by the *Konjaku* compiler is 57. Gjertson, *Ming-pao chi*, p. 190. I have translated only one example of these stories (7:18); the correspondence between a *Konjaku* and a *Ming-pao chi* version of the same story is as a rule extremely close. The most common topic is a visit to hell, generally envisioned in terms of the Chinese judicial bureaucracy.

9. Translations of a few tales from the *Hokke genki* appear in Dykstra, "Miraculous Tales." Two of these have rather close parallels with stories in my selection from *Konjaku*: the story of Shunchō (*Hokke genki* 1:22) is the obvious source for KM 13:10; and that of the government clerk of Higo province (3:110) for KM 12:28. But note how, in the latter, the *Konjaku* compiler prolongs the conversation between the ogre at the mouth of the cave and

bosatsu reigenki (1016–1068),[10] which are anthologies of *setsuwa*
intended to promote the worship of particular bodhisattvas or
sutras. There is still much controversy among Japanese scholars,
however, as to where *exactly* the compiler found his material. To
what degree, even in drawing on written works, was he dependent on someone's retelling? To what degree, when he wrote from
oral tradition, was that oral tradition itself dependent on written
texts, many of which may not have survived? But it seems fairly
clear that the sources of the stories in the first twenty chapters
were predominantly written, while the secular anecdotes of
Japan rely predominantly on oral tradition. (The poem-tales in
chapter 30 may be an exception.) Where he had written texts
before him, he followed them faithfully, on the whole. Sometimes, as in the tale of the three beasts, he would supply detail,
and always he would adapt the beginning and end to his formulaic requirements. But often he did little more than translate
from the Chinese; and throughout the first ten chapters the style
is that of a very minimal sort of translation. From the middle
chapters on, however, the language, though inelegant by courtly
standards, is a much purer Japanese; the storytelling is altogether
freer and livelier; and whether the stories should be called the
responsibility of one compiler or of many compilers plus the
other hands they had passed through, it becomes possible to talk
about them with some confidence in terms of a consistent taste
and consistent attitudes, perhaps even — if to do so is not making
altogether too much of a work in a humble genre — of artistry.

One thing that is particularly striking is the aloofness of the
narrator. He often expresses admiration for a character on the
score of cleverness and prudence or of piety; and we are likely to
have some fellow-feeling for the protagonist of a story because we
all share the human condition and are all alike on the edge of the
abyss, will in fact all tumble over it if we do not learn what he has
just learned. But the characters are generally seen at a distance
and are not accorded sympathy unless they have done something
to earn it. Where there are exceptions, there is generally a reason:

the voice within the cave — and instead of having the terrified fugitive merely
guess that the voice within the cave is also that of an ogre has the speaker
explicitly impersonate an ogre.

10. See Dykstra, "Jizō," for a selection. Among those stories translated, its
1:5 parallels, although not closely, KM 17:2.

the story of the reed-cutter in Chapter Thirty (story 5) is still bound to the lyrical tradition of its original genre, while the young couple who escape the bandit in Chapter Sixteen are figures from a sentimental convention. One of the finest stories in all of *Konjaku,* that of a neglectful lover who becomes the victim of his dead mistress (31:7), does indeed seem to indulge in psychological probings; but this invitation to empathy is a deception, intended to deepen the shock when, in the end, the sinful man gets no less than he deserves.

The compiler's skepticism about appearances extends to human nature and human motives. One good example is the story of an eminent monk who seems fatally ill. His disciples are told by a diviner that their master can be saved only if one of them will give up his own life in his place (19:24). None will volunteer; finally a disciple to whom no one had ever paid much attention steps forward. In the end, not only is his master saved, but the disciple himself is spared. The legend itself must have been widely known; it is referred to, for example, in the early fourteenth-century memoir *Towazugatari*.[11] As it appears in other *setsuwa* collections (for example *Hōbutsushū,* ca. 1178–1179, and *Hosshinshū,* ca. 1215–1216) and in a history of Japanese Buddhism, *Genkō shakusho* (1322), the story is propaganda for the cult of Fudō, who in turn takes on the suffering of his devotee. *Konjaku* eschews this doctrinal point entirely, so that the ending, which says only that divine powers took pity on the hero, is rather weak, giving the impression that the hard bargain was a test, not a bargain, and that the hero is simply being let off the hook.[12] But it makes much of the avarice of the other, higher-ranking disciples, which is not mentioned in other versions, and the result is a quite wonderful scene in which the disciples sit looking at each other, each rather hoping that someone else might be moved to volunteer, but at the same time nursing thoughts of the nice inheritance that will result if no one does.

The narrator's coolness can at times produce a fine balance of

11. Karen Brazell, trans., *The Confessions of Lady Nijō* (Garden City, New York: Doubleday Anchor, 1973), p. 13, 246–247.

12. The name of the hero of this anecdote appears in *Towazugatari,* and other versions in which he is helped by Fudō, as Shōkū. As this name was unknown to the compiler of *Konjaku,* it is possible that he was acquainted with a somewhat different form of the legend. But in any event it is clear that it is not the resolution of the story that holds his chief attention.

ironies. An upstart monk becomes violently jealous of an eminent Buddhist master and physically evicts him from the pulpit
(20:35). The upstart is a wretch, and his horrible fate thereafter
amply demonstrates the principle of karmic retribution. But the
worthy man whom he has abused is, though no hypocrite, one
whose conversion to a life of contemplation had certainly been
convenient, coming at the very moment that his opportunities
for secular amusement were exhausted. The brisk recital of the
circumstances of his religious awakening might almost be a par-
ody of the accounts of the conversion experiences in Chapter
Nineteen.[13] It is clear that we need not waste our sympathy on
him; his discomfiture is not shocking but funny. Nor are we
invited to sympathize with the true losers in all this, those who
hired him; perhaps because that is the sort of thing that people
who make pretentious plans are letting themselves in for.

The same coolness governs the compiler's admiration. The
comment has been made that when the action of a story is dependent on more than one character, it is sometimes hard to know
which to call the protagonist.[14] A husband catches his wife's
lover and quietly locks him in a chest; the lover maintains the
presence of mind to utter a witty remark at the embarrassing
moment when he must emerge from the chest in front of his own
subordinates (28:11).[15] The compiler scarcely knows whom to
commend more: the husband for not creating a scene and for
keeping his wits about him, or the lover for preserving the one
thing he can — his reputation for a ready tongue — in the midst of
humiliation.

13. By conversion is meant a change of heart leading to a life of meditation
and devotion; the convert may be a layman, or he may already be a monk. An
example of a conversion story in my translation is 19:8; others may be found
in Kelsey, "Konjaku"; and, from a later text, in Ury, "Recluses and Eccentric
Monks: Tales from the *Hosshinshū* by Kamo no Chōmei," *Monumenta Nipponica,* 27 (1972), 149–174.

14. Nagano Jōichi, "*Konjaku monogatari* to kindai sakka," *Kokubungaku:
Kaishaku to kanshō,*" vol. 24, no. 7 (June 1959), pp. 10–18. In some stories, I
might suggest, we have a division of roles very similar to that in the *nō* drama.
There is the traveler who witnesses the crucial happening; he corresponds to
the *waki,* or deuteragonist, of the *nō.* And there is the character who experiences or performs it, corresponding to the protagonist in the *nō.* An example
would be the story of the outcaste monk, 15:28.

15. Among all the stories translated — perhaps among all the stories in *Konjaku* — this is the one that seems to bear the most resemblance to Boccaccio.

Konjaku was compiled at a time of social change. In the capital, the system of aristocratic rule, which had been in its glory a hundred years earlier, was under strain, while in the provinces the military families which by the end of the century would provide the de facto rulers of Japan were gathering strength. Japanese critics are fond of raising the question of the compiler's social sympathies. Although there is a chapter devoted to tales of warriors (like the one devoted to the Fujiwara, it is very short and may be incomplete), its subjects are viewed less as a special class with distinctive ideals than as virtuosi; with special skills, to be true, and their own professional code, but not so very different, for all that, from other men of accomplishment like sumō wrestlers and masters of Chinese poetry. As for social class: persons of humble station are heroes of a number of stories and are shown possessing desirable qualities and behaving in praiseworthy ways. But they can also be made butts of humor. Rustics, no matter how worthy, are easily made fun of, as are underofficials, who are repeatedly depicted offending against the canons of good sense and good taste.[16]

Provincial governors, proverbially greedy, inspire detestation or laughter, depending on the story. Stirrings of social consciousness of the modern sort have been detected in an account of a group of lower-ranking civil servants, imperial guardsmen, who picket the Kyoto mansion of a governor who has misappropriated their pay (28:5); alas for this theory, the governor ultimately wins out through a ruse, to the entertainment not only of the compiler but of the protesters themselves, who cheerfully admit that they have been outsmarted. A social critic ought to take the plight of the injured seriously, but here even the victims themselves are not allowed to do so. If consistency is to be found, it should be sought not in attitudes toward specific classes but in the compiler's liking for persons, of whatever class, who can cope, and in his sound narrative instincts.

The social changes of the century that followed the compila-

But it is also unlike Boccaccio. For one thing, the illicit sexual relationship only provides the *occasion* here. More important, there are no real winners: what each of the men is praised for by the compiler is having cut his losses.

16. One example is 28:30, which has a parallel in *Uji shūi monogatari*; for a translation see Mills, pp. 168–170.

tion of *Konjaku* were accompanied by important new develop-
ments in Japanese religion: the rise and spread of the belief in
calling on the name of the Buddha Amida as the sole practical
means of salvation, and the first meaningful importation of Zen;
and the century following that saw the rise and spread of an
intolerant Lotus Sutra cult. But devotion to Amida is only one of a
number of Buddhist religious practices that appear in *Konjaku*,
and his cult is only one of a number that are all recommended
with impartial enthusiasm. In the story of the outcaste saint
(15:28), for example, the saint is shown worshipping the Lotus
Sutra; but at the hour of his death he faces west, in the posture of
an Amidist devotee, and the miraculous omens that are witnessed
by the visitor are typical of those that attest to a rebirth in
Amida's paradise.

The dominant beliefs in *Konjaku* are found within the broad
teachings of the Tendai school, from which the later, exclusive
sects were to arise. As do those of other Mahayana schools, they
include the belief that Śākyamuni, the founder of Buddhism, was
one of a succession of Buddhas and bodhisattvas, eternal beings
that manifest themselves on earth or preside over paradises, for
the salvation of all sentient beings. But even though his life is the
principal subject of the India chapters of *Konjaku*, Śākyamuni
himself was not a popular focus of devotion in Japan; more popular by far, along with Amida, were Kannon (Avalokiteśvara), who
comes to the aid of worshippers in distress, and Jizō (Kṣitigarbha),
who rescues sinners from hell and who, in Japan, often appears
among men in the guise of a small boy or a young monk. But these
are only a few of the divine beings in *Konjaku*. Even such Indian
gods as Brahma and Indra were enrolled by Buddhism to act as
protectors of the Buddha's teaching, his Dharma.

Konjaku presents a variety of religious beliefs existing side by
side; sometimes there was conscious syncretism, but mostly, one
suspects, people simply entertained all of them without asking
whether they were strictly consonant with one another.
Śākyamuni is shown promoting the Confucian virtue of filial
piety (2:1); the disciples of a Buddhist master who is mortally ill
summon a Taoist diviner, who questions the Chinese deity who
presides over the Taoist afterworld (19:24); a wealthy layman who
has been bewitched by foxes is saved through the grace of Kannon, whereupon his relatives call in a Taoist doctor and a Bud-

dhist exorcist in the hope of speeding his restoration to health
(16:17). Native belief provided a lively repertory of bogies and
ogres, to join and blend with one of continental origin. Shinto was
scarcely thought of at this time as a separate religion. The Buddhist monks in the celebrated Dōjōji story (14:3) are on their way
to vist a Shinto shrine. The troublesome demonic deities in the
story of E no Ubasoku (11:3) are Shinto divinities of a sort; he has
mastered them through the spells of tantric Buddhism, but they
accuse him through a native shaman, and when he is captured, it
is because of the imperative demands of filial piety.

Some word is owed the reader on the principles governing the
selection, translation, and annotation of the stories in the present
volume. A good deal might be said in favor of a selection that
would consist of long sequences from several chapters, but since
the only previous translation in English that attempts to represent the varied subject matter of the whole book is unsatisfactory
on several counts, I have chosen rather to make a selection that
would suggest something of the dimensions of *Konjaku* in the
large. Unlike Bernard Frank, whose French translation I very
much admire, I have not attempted to follow the structure of the
original in detail; I have, however, chosen at least one story from
each chapter. I have tried to illustrate a variety of styles and
themes. Beyond that, I have made literary value a major criterion
in selection—perhaps this is no more than to say that I have
translated stories which, for one reason or another, I especially
liked. I am sensible of the loss in choosing stories without attention to sequences. Whether sequence invariably contributes to
the value of the individual story, I would question. Nevertheless,
repetition of an element from story to story often serves to
sharpen the focus on it in each story. In a number of instances,
therefore, I have provided both members of a pair of linked
stories. (There are also, fortuitously, a few examples of stories
adjacent to each other without strong links.)

Since so much of *Konjaku* remains to be translated, it was my
original intention to avoid choosing stories that had already appeared in competent Western-language renderings. This has not
always been possible. Most of the better translations are not very
readily obtainable; moreover, it seemed unfair to deprive my own
readers, in this cause, of the beginning and end of the book. My

intention, however, has also been to add to the corpus of *setsuwa* generally that are available in Western-language translation. Where possible, I have refrained from translating stories that have close parallels in other works that have been translated; this explains the relative paucity of stories from Chapter Seven, as well as the absence of any of the *tengu* stories from Chapter Twenty (the best of these are duplicated in *Uji shūi monogatari*). Where I have broken this rule, it has been with the thought that scholars might find the opportunity to compare two ways of telling the same story instructive. Finally, I have tried to avoid stories that would require paraphrasing or excessive amounts of annotation to be made intelligible.

Although I would hope that this translation might be of some use to scholars, the readers whom I have principally in mind are simply all those who, like myself, are fond of stories and are interested in how they are told. In translating longer fiction one might — perhaps always *should* — be prepared to work with some freedom; but translating very short stories can be a different matter entirely. Much of the effectiveness of the telling may depend upon very small moments of suspense, precise proportions, even the minute sequence of revelations within the order of a single sentence. I have tried to do as little violence to these things as possible. Throughout, I have been as literal as I dared: that is to say, somewhat more so in the first ten chapters, corresponding to the compiler's own literalness in handling his own sources, and somewhat less so in the final ones; unavoidably much less so in rendering dialogue, since Japanese, like English-speakers, tend to converse in fragments of sentences — only not in the same fragments. The result is a style with considerable variations; these do in fact correspond in some measure to variations in the original. The general imagelessness of the original prose is striking, making the few exceptions stand out all the more vividly; I have been at some pains not to introduce images of my own, even — or especially — of the "dead metaphor" variety.

Konjaku is full of repetitions: phrases that might be translated "so seeing," "so hearing," "so saying" occur time after time, in passages in which it is already obvious that the thing is seen, heard, or said; and when someone reports to someone the contents of a conversation with someone else he almost invariably does it in full. Such repetitions are one of the devices, primitive but effective, for regulating the pace of the storytelling, and although I have often succumbed to the temptation to delete short phrases of the first sort even when translating most literally, I have preserved as much of the other sort of repetition as I thought readers could be induced to bear. Classical Japanese in general tolerates repetition and a limited vocabulary much better than does English—or for that matter modern Japanese. The text abounds in set phrases such as *kagiri nashi,* literally "unbounded" or "without limit." (S. W. Jones, imagining the style of the original to be more peculiar than it actually is, translates this pertly "no end.") There are good arguments for translating such expressions unvaryingly throughout, as several others have done; I have chosen not to, however, my grounds being that such practice makes the phrases seem altogether more important than they deserve to be. Although naturalness in English has not been my first consideration, I have tried not to sound unnecessarily quaint or odd.

The intentional lacunae have been a problem; no doubt the easiest solution, as well as the most respectable, would be to reproduce each blank in the Japanese with a blank in English. But the blanks are a great deal more obtrusive in English than in Japanese: in Japanese they seem to signal that there is information that will be supplied; in English they signal all too strongly that it is lacking. In English they may seem pedantic; unless the translator is very cautious indeed, they can become inadvertently comic. Where I could—again, I have not been able to be consistent—I adopted the device of filling in the lacuna with some noncommittal word or phrase and enclosing my emendation in brackets. Many objections might be made against this practice, but it does preserve the flow of the story, and those who find it offensive are welcome to replace mentally the bracketed passages with suitable blanks. Sometimes the information which the compiler originally lacked is now obtainable, but a case might be made for not making ourselves too much wiser than the original readers, and I have therefore mostly refrained from using it in the translation itself. Lacunae resulting from the compiler's orthographic problems (according to one modern editor, Mabuchi Kazuo, he sometimes left a space when he could not think of the appropriate character for a word) or from physical damage I have emended silently where little guesswork was involved; for major lacunae that result from physical damage to the manuscripts there is not much remedy. In transcribing personal and place names I have followed the readings given by Yamada Yoshio et al. in the *taikei* edition (see Select Bibliography); where I thought these might confuse readers familiar with differing modern forms, I have mentioned the latter in the notes.

Since this translation is meant for the general reader, I have kept annotation to the minimum; as it is, there are probably too many notes for the taste of many readers. For the benefit of those who may be new to the subject, I have explained a very few of the elementary notions of Buddhism; following my own whim, in a few places I have discussed more technical matters. But I realize that there is a vast, neglected area in between. I can only ask my readers to learn from the stories themselves, as the original audience did. Modern Japanese readers of *Konjaku* are much interested in the places mentioned in it, and rightfully so, but place-name identifications are not always very meaningful to Western readers, and I have thus annotated place names only when, in my judgment, the information had some likelihood of enhancing an understanding of the events in the story. The subject of the sources of the individual stories and their variants is a fascinating one, but a very complex one, and even to begin to deal adequately with it would require a volume many times the length of the present book. I hope I may be forgiven for having discussed them only in a few instances.

A NOTE ON TEXTS

For several centuries after its compilation, *Konjaku* seems not to have been widely known. Its title is not mentioned in any other book until 1451. There is only one premodern printed edition, a curious and corrupt partial one, edited by Izawa Nagahide and printed in Kyoto in 1720; a copy of it in the collection of the East Asiatic Library of the University of California, Berkeley, is the source of my illustrations. The present translation is based on the complete text in the *Nihon koten bungaku taikei* series; otherwise unacknowledged commentarial opinion cited in the notes to my translations is usually that of its editors. The Select Bibliography lists this and other editions (including translations into modern Japanese) that I have consulted and found especially helpful, along with partial translations and studies in Western languages of *Konjaku* and of related texts that seemed especially pertinent; it does not pretend to be a complete bibliography on *setsuwa* in Western languages, and it omits a number of brief items on *Konjaku*. To those who know modern Japanese, I can strongly recommend the translation by Nagazumi and Ikegami, which is lively, meticulous, and usefully annotated. For a comprehensive account of research on *Konjaku* through the 1950s, an article by Nishio Kōichi, "*Konjaku monogatari* kenkyūshi" in *Kokubungaku: Kaishaku to kanshō,* vol. 24, no. 7 (June 1959), pp. 51–63, is also highly recommended. There are a number of useful bibliographies in Japanese of *setsuwa* in general and *Konjaku* in particular; of these I might mention especially the annotated list in *Setsuwa bungaku hikkei,* ed. Hinotani Akihiko, Kobayashi Yasuharu, and Takahashi Mitsugu, in the series *Nihon no setsuwa* (Tokyo: Tōkyō bijutsu, 1976).

Select Bibliography

TEXTS

Haga Yaichi, ed. *Kōshō Konjaku monogatari shū.* 3 vols. Tokyo: Fuzanbō, 1913–1921. A pioneering printing of the complete text, together with variants and possible sources of each story.

Mabuchi Kazuo, Kunisaki Fumimaro, and Konno Tōru, eds. *Konjaku monogatari shū.* Nihon koten bungaku zenshū, vols. 21–24. Tokyo: Shōgakkan, 1971–1976. Text, with modern Japanese translation, of chapters 11–31.

Nagano Jōichi, ed. *Konjaku monogatari.* Nihon koten zensho, 6 vols. Tokyo: Asahi Shinbunsha, 1953–1957. Chapters 11–31 only.

Nagazumi Yasuaki and Ikegami Jun'ichi, trans. *Konjaku monogatari shū.* 6 vols. Tokyo: Heibonsha, 1966–1968. Chapters 11–31 only.

Yamada Yoshio, Yamada Tadao, Yamada Hideo, and Yamada Toshio, eds. *Konjaku monogatari shū.* Nihon koten bungaku taikei, vols. 22–26. Tokyo: Iwanami Shoten, 1965 (1st ed. 1959–1963).

TRANSLATIONS AND STUDIES IN WESTERN LANGUAGES

Brower, Robert H. "The *Koñzyaku monogatarisyū.*" Ph.D. dissertation, University of Michigan, 1952. Contains translations of 78 stories from chapters 11–31.

Dykstra, Yoshiko Kurata. "Jizō, the Most Merciful: Tales from *Jizō Bosatsu Reigenki.*" *Monumenta Nipponica,* 33 (1978), 179–200.

———. "Miraculous Tales of the Lotus Sutra: The *Dainihonkoku Hokkegenki.*" *Monumenta Nipponica,* 32 (1977), 189–210.

————."Tales of the Compassionate Kannon: The *Hasedera Kannon Genki.*" *Monumenta Nipponica,* 31 (1976), 113–143.

Frank, Bernard. *Histoires qui sont maintenant du passé.* Paris: Gallimard, 1968. Translations of 58 stories from *Konjaku* with extensive annotation.

Gjertson, Donald E. "A Study and Translation of the *Ming-pao chi:* a T'ang Dynasty Collection of Tales." Ph.D. dissertation, Stanford University, 1975.

Hammitsch, Horst, ed. *Erzählungen des alten Japan aus dem Konjaku monogatari.* Trans. Ingrid Schuster and Klaus Müller. Stuttgart: Reclam, 1965. 23 stories from chapters 17–31.

Jones, S. W. *Ages Ago: Thirty-Seven Tales from the Konjaku Monogatari Collection.* Cambridge, Mass.: Harvard University Press, 1959.

Kelsey, W. Michael, "*Konjaku Monogatari-shū:* Toward an Understanding of Its Literary Qualities." *Monumenta Nipponica,* 30 (1975), 121–150. Translation and analysis of four tales of religious conversion, from chapter 19.

Mills, D. E. *A Collection of Tales from Uji: A Study and Translation of Uji Shūi Monogatari.* Cambridge University Press, 1970.

Nakamura, Kyoko Motomochi, trans. *Miraculous Stories from the Japanese Buddhist Tradition: The Nihon ryōiki of the Monk Kyōkai.* Cambridge, Mass.: Harvard University Press, 1973.

Tsukakoshi, Satoshi, trans. *Konjaku: Altjapanische Geschichten aus dem Volk zur Heian-Zeit.* Zurich: Max Niehans, 1956. 42 stories from chapters 22–31.

Wilson, William Ritchie. "The Way of the Bow and Arrow: The Japanese Warrior in *Konjaku Monogatari.*" *Monumenta Nipponica,* 28 (1973), 177–233. Annotated translation of chapter 25.

KONJAKU MONOGATARI SHŪ

Tales of India

The first eight tales in Chapter One form a sequence that narrates the life of the historical Buddha, from his conception and birth to the time of his first sermon; the last eight tales in Chapter Three similarly form a sequence that tells of his death as a man and his obsequies. The translation includes the first and last stories in the former sequence and the first in the latter (1:1, 1:8, 3:28). In between are accounts of other events in the life of Śākyamuni, events that illustrate his teachings. The doctrinal message in these stories is generally of the simplest, intended to be understood by ordinary believers; a major concern is the karmic rewards to be earned by charity, especially as practiced toward the Buddha and the monastic community. Nāgārjuna and Bodhidharma, whose stories appear in Chapter Four, are among the most renowned patriarchs of later Buddhism. The Japanese knew India almost exclusively as the land in which Buddhism originated, but such traditions as they possessed in regard to the secular history of the region are recorded in Chapter Five; its Story 2 is one of a pair which, in quite different ways, describe the founding of Ceylon and explain its name. The legend of the rabbit in the moon, which appears in the same chapter, is one that enjoys perennial popularity in Japan.

Chapter One

1. HOW ŚĀKYAMUNI TATHĀGATA CAME TO DWELL IN THE WORLD OF MEN

AT A TIME NOW PAST, when Śākyamuni Tathāgata was not yet Buddha, he was called Śākyamuni Bodhisattva and dwelled in the Inner Court of the Tuṣita heaven.[1] When the time came that he determined to be born upon earth, he manifested the five signs of mortal decay. The five signs of a divine being's mortal decay are namely these: first, the eyes of the gods do not blink, but he blinks; second, the garlands on the heads of the gods do not wither, but his garlands wither; third, no dust adheres to the clothing of the gods, but dust and dirt settle on him; fourth, the gods do not perspire, but he exudes perspiration under his arms; fifth, a god never changes his seat, but he, without seeking out his own seat, sits down wherever he may be.

The gods all saw the Bodhisattva manifest these signs, and they spoke to him in wonder and apprehension, saying: "Today we have seen you manifest the signs of decay. Our bodies tremble and our minds are bewildered. Tell us the reason, we pray you."

The Buddha replied, "Know that all phenomenal existence is impermanent. Soon I shall leave these heavenly mansions to be reborn on the continent of Jambudvīpa."[2] Hearing this, the gods all uttered lamentations.

The Buddha then thought, "Whom shall I choose to be my father and whom my mother when I am born on earth?" He decided, "Śuddhodana, King of Kapilavastu, and Queen Māyā are entirely fit to be made my parents."

On the eighth day of the seventh month of a *mizunoto-ushi* year,[3] he lodged in the womb of Queen Māyā. As the Queen lay sleeping in the night, she dreamed that the Bodhisattva descended from the skies riding upon a white elephant with six tusks, and that he entered her body through her right side. Her body was transparent, and he was visible through it, like an object inside a beryl jar. The Queen awoke with a start. She went to the King and told him her dream. "I too," said the King, "have had such a dream. Unaided, I cannot interpret it." He forthwith summoned a Brahman skilled in the reading of omens. He made the Brahman offerings of finely fragrant flowers and various sorts of food and drink and asked him about the vision the Queen had seen in her dream. The Brahman said to the King, "The prince whom the Queen has conceived is marked with every marvelous and excellent sign. I cannot explain all the particulars, but to you, O King, I shall tell it in brief. The child within the Queen's womb is one that only the brilliant race of the Śākyas could produce. At the time that he issues from the womb, he will emit a great light. Brahma and Indra and all the gods will pay him homage. These felicitous omens show without a doubt that he is to become Buddha. If, perchance, he does not renounce secular life, however, he will become a universal sage king; he will fill the four continents with precious substances and be blessed with a thousand sons."

Hearing the Brahman's prophecy, the King felt boundless joy. He gave the Brahman precious goods of every kind, gold and silver, elephants and horses and carriages; and the Queen, too, gave him vast treasure. The Brahman received the precious gifts that the King and Queen bestowed on him and returned whence he had come. So the tale's been told, and so it's been handed down.

Notes to Story 1

1. Tathāgata is an epithet borne by the Buddha after enlightenment. The Inner Court of the Tuṣita heaven is where the future Buddha dwells while awaiting final reincarnation upon earth. (There is also an Outer Court where gods dwell.) For the heavens in general, see 1:11, note 2.

2. In Buddhist cosmology, the southernmost of the continents surrounding the world mountain; the word is sometimes used synonymously with India, sometimes just to denote the world of men.

3. *Mizunoto-ushi:* the fiftieth year in a cycle of sixty. This method of counting years is a Chinese and Japanese, not an Indian, one.

8. HOW ŚĀKYAMUNI PREACHED
THE DHARMA TO FIVE BHIKSHUS

AT A TIME NOW PAST, Śākyamuni Tathāgata went to the country of Benares, to a place where five bhikshus[1] were residing, Kaundinya among them. From afar the five men saw him come; and they said to each other, "The śramana Gautama has given up self-torment and comes here now to be given food. We need not rise to greet him." But when the Tathāgata had come, each man got up from his seat and greeted him with reverent salutation. Thereupon the Tathāgata addressed them: "O ye of little wisdom, be not disdainful; do not doubt that I have achieved the Way. And as to the reason: the practice of self-torment deludes and confuses the mind, while partaking of pleasure addicts the heart[2] to pleasure. I therefore have left the two ways of pain and pleasure to follow the middle Way; and now I have succeeded in attaining bodhi." And the Tathāgata preached to the five men the Four Truths of Suffering, the Origin of Suffering, the Extinction of Suffering, and the Way for the Extinction of Suffering. Hearing this sermon, the five men were freed of defilement and rid of pain and acquired the clear vision of the Dharma eye.[3] Now about the five men: their names were (one) Kaundinya, (two) Mahākāśyapa, (three) Aśvajit, (four) Bhadrika, (five) Mahānāman. Should it be asked, "Why was it these five men?" the answer is that long, long ago, in the age in which Kāśyapa was the Buddha, there were nine fellow-scholars. Four were clever and attained the Way from the very beginning; the five men whose wits were dull . . .[4] only later became enlightened. They vowed to be reborn at the time when Śākyamuni would appear in the world and achieve the Way. So the tale's been handed down.

Notes to Story 8

1. The term bhikshu is used in this story in the general sense of ascetic religious practitioner, although ordinarily it is one of several essentially synonymous terms for a member of the Buddhist religious order; the point here is that the five men are not yet converts. Sramana, in Buddhist texts, likewise ordinarily refers to a member of the Buddhist order, but it can also refer to ascetic practitioners of all persuasions in India. The appellation Gautama which the five men use for the Buddha

has overtones of contempt here, because it is a surname borne by the Buddha *before* he became enlightened; see also the next story.

2. "Heart" and "mind" both render the same word, *kokoro.*

3. Clear vision of the Dharma eye: *dharmacakṣurviśuddha,* the ability to discern the Truth, the result of hearing the Dharma.

4. Lacuna owing to damage to the text.

11. HOW THE BUDDHA ENTERED A CITY OF THE BRAHMANS TO BEG FOOD

AT A TIME NOW PAST, the Buddha decided to enter a city of the Brahmans to beg his food. The heathen in that city were all of one mind against him. "Lately this bhikshu Gautama, as he is called, has been going from house to house and begging things to eat," one said to another. "He is ill-favored and hateful. He was once of exalted station; he was the son of King Śuddhodana and he ought to have inherited his father's throne, but for no apparent reason he went mad, they say, went into the mountains, and became Buddha. He addles men's minds, and there are many here whom he has taken in. On no account should he be given alms." A decree was circulated: "Whoever breaks the covenant and makes him an offering shall be driven from the kingdom." After that, when the Buddha went for alms, he found at some houses that the gates were bolted, at other houses he waited and waited without an answer, and at yet others the inhabitants told him to be gone and drove him away. As this was the manner of his reception, he failed to gain any alms before the sun rose high.[1] Looking famished, his empty bowl pressed against his breast, he was returning to his dwelling when a woman came out of one of the houses to throw away putrid water in which some days previously rice had been washed. Seeing the Buddha returning without offerings, she was moved to pity. "If only I might give him something!" she thought, but she was poor and had nothing at all to offer. "What can I do?" she thought, and her eyes swam with tears. The Buddha saw her standing there. "What grieves you?" he asked. "I saw that the Buddha had gained no alms before the sun rose high," she replied, "and I thought, if only I might offer him something! But my household is poor, and I have nothing at all to give. That is why I grieve," and her tears fell as she spoke. "What is in the pail you carry?" asked the Buddha. "Spoiled rice-water that I am taking to throw away." The Buddha said, "Rather, give it to me. It is wholesome food, for it has the taste of rice." "A strange thing indeed you ask," said the woman, "but I shall obey," and she filled his bowl. The Buddha raised it in his hands and pronounced a blessing: "Through the merit of this act, when you are reborn among the gods it shall be as king of the Trayastriṁśa heaven,[2] and when you are reborn among men it shall also be as a king. Such is the infinite merit of this act."

One of the heathen had gone to the top of a tower and from there had seen how the Buddha was driven from house to house, how he received no offering before the sun was high, how he was going away famished, and how he took the putrid liquid the woman was discarding and blessed it. The unbeliever came out and ridiculed him: "Buddha, why do you deceive men with such lies? This is no wholesome food; it is putrid liquid that she was taking to throw away. Yet, when some comes into your hands, you say that the giver will be reborn in heaven or as a king among men. That is a monstrous lie!" The Buddha said, "Have you seen the seed of the banyan tree?" "Yes, I have," said the heathen. The Buddha said, "How large is it?" The heathen said, "It is even smaller than a grain of mustard." The Buddha said, "And how large is the banyan tree?" The heathen said, "It can shelter five hundred carriages under its branches and have shade to spare." The Buddha said, "By this example you shall understand. The tree born of a seed smaller than a grain of mustard can shelter five hundred carriages and have shade to spare. The merit that springs from the slightest offering to the Buddha is incalculable. Your actions in this world are like the seed; know then that your reward in afterlives is like the tree." When the heathen heard this he was overcome with awe and did homage to the Buddha; the hair dropped from his head spontaneously, and thus tonsured, he became an arhat.[3] The woman, too, upon hearing the Buddha's prophecy performed reverent salutations; and she departed. So the tale's been told, and so it's been handed down.

Notes to Story 11

1. Buddhist monks were forbidden to eat after noon.

2. Early Buddhism believed that above the world-mountain there were six heavens of the gods; of these the most often mentioned was the Trayastriṁśa heaven (Japanese, Tōriten), ruled over by Indra, and the Tuṣita heaven (Japanese, Tosotten), where Maitreya, the Buddha of the future, now awaits his time on earth. The disadvantage of being reborn as a god in one of the heavens is, as we shall find in the next story, that life in them, though long, was not everlasting. Belief in these heavens persisted in Japan alongside the newer belief in the Pureland paradise established by the Buddha Amitabha (Amida).

3. An arhat may be defined as one who has experienced enlightenment, inferior only to the Buddha himself; in use the term often denotes the direct disciples of the Buddha. The arhat was freed from further rebirth — again an important point in the story that follows.

18. HOW THE BUDDHA CONVERTED NANDA AND CAUSED HIM TO RENOUNCE SECULAR LIFE

AT A TIME NOW PAST, there was among the Buddha's disciples a man called Nanda. Formerly, as a householder, he had had a wife who was the most beautiful woman in all the five Indias. Clinging to his love for her, he did not believe in the Buddha's teaching and he ignored the Buddha's chiding. At the time of this story, the Buddha was residing in a grove of fig trees; in company with his disciple Ānanda, he went to Nanda's house to convert him. Nanda had climbed to the top of a tower and saw from afar the Buddha begging with his bowl. Nanda hurried down from the tower and went to the Buddha, saying: "You, my Lord, were born to be a universal sage king. How is it that you are not ashamed to beg your food?" And taking the bowl in his own hands, he went into his house, filled it with delicious food and drink, and returned with it to the Buddha. The Buddha would not accept it. Returning to the grove of fig trees, he told Nanda: "If you will renounce secular life, then I will accept the bowl." Nanda heard this and prepared to present the bowl in accordance with the

Buddha's words. His wife came out and said, "Come home soon."
With the intent of renouncing secular life, Nanda went to where
the Buddha was living and presented the bowl; he said, "I pray
you, accept this." The Buddha said to Nanda, "Now that you are
here, shave your head and put on religious dress. Do not think of
returning to your home." With his supernatural powers the Buddha had assailed Nanda; now he had Ānanda ordain him. And so,
Nanda remained in the abode of purity; the Buddha gradually
soothed him, and he rejoiced.[1]

Now Nanda still cherished the wish to visit his wife. While
the Buddha was away he tried to go to her; but the door he was
going to go out by suddenly closed. Another door opened, but
when he tried to go out through that door, it closed and another
opened. Thus, he could not go out—and then the Buddha returned, and he could not go out.[2] On another occasion he
thought, "If only the Buddha would absent himself a short while!
During that time I would go to my wife." The Buddha announced that he was going somewhere and gave Nanda a broom.
"Sweep here," he said. Nanda busied himself so as to be done
quickly with the sweeping, but a wind arose from nowhere and
blew all the dust back. Before he could finish, the Buddha returned. Yet again, when the Buddha had gone somewhere, Nanda
left the monks' chambers, thinking: "During this interval I will
go to my wife. The Buddha will surely return by the same road."
But the Buddha knew, without being told, exactly what was in
Nanda's mind, and he returned by the road that Nanda took.
When Nanda from afar saw the Buddha approach, he hid at the
foot of a great tree. The spirit of the tree suddenly raised the tree
into the air and exposed him. The Buddha saw Nanda and es-
corted him back to the monastery. In such manner was Nanda
kept from returning to his wife.

The Buddha said to Nanda, "Study the Way. You pay no heed to
the afterlife; now that is extremely foolish. I shall go with you
and show you the heavens." So declaring, he ascended with him
to the Trayastriṁśa heaven. He exhibited the heavenly palaces
where the gods and goddesses enjoy their boundless pleasures.
Inside one of the palaces, Nanda saw precious ornaments, too
many to count. Within this palace were five hundred goddesses
and no gods. Nanda asked the Buddha, "Why are there only
female deities in this palace?" The Buddha asked a goddess, and

she replied, "On earth there is a man named Nanda who is a disciple of the Buddha. Recently he renounced secular life. Owing to the merit of this act, when his life is over he will be reborn in this heavenly palace. It is because he is to be the god that there is no male deity here." When Nanda heard this, he thought, "Why, that's I myself!" The Buddha said to him, "Can your wife rival the goddess in beauty?" Nanda said, "When I compare my wife in my mind with the goddess, my wife looks like a monkey. But then, so do I." Having seen the goddess, Nanda suddenly forgot all about his wife. He scrupulously adhered to the monastic vows in the hope of being reborn here.

On another occasion the Buddha took Nanda to hell. Their path traversed the iron mountains that ring the world. On the other side of the mountains were beings called monkey-women, who were incomparably beautiful. Among them was one called Sundarī. Nanda saw her. The Buddha said, "Can your wife rival Sundarī? Is she as fine as this monkey-woman?" Nanda said, "Were my wife a hundred, a thousand times more beautiful, the two could still not be compared." The Buddha said, "Again, can Sundarī vie with the goddesses?" Nanda said, "Were Sundarī a thousand, ten thousand times more beautiful there would be no comparison." The Buddha and Nanda arrived in hell. The Buddha showed Nanda all sorts of cauldrons. They were full of boiling water, and people were being cooked in them. Nanda was terrified at the sight. But he saw one cauldron boiling away with nobody in it. Nanda asked one of the demons, "Why isn't anyone in this pot?" The demon replied, "On earth there is a disciple of the Buddha named Nanda who, owing to the merit of renouncing secular life, will be reborn in heaven. Ultimately, his span of life in heaven will be exhausted, and he will drop into hell. I blow the fires high under this cauldron because I wait for Nanda." Nanda was filled with dread. He said to the Buddha, "Please take me back to earth at once. Protect me!" The Buddha said to Nanda, "Observe well your vows, that you may obtain the felicities of heaven." "I no longer want to be reborn in heaven," said Nanda; "just don't drop me into hell."

The Buddha and Nanda returned to earth, and for Nanda's sake the Buddha in the space of seven days preached the Dharma and caused him to achieve the fruits of arhatship. So the tale's been told, and so it's been handed down.

Notes to Story 18

1. It has been suggested that Nanda is rejoicing in anticipation of re-union with his wife, as other versions of the story explicitly state. The compiler of *Konjaku* seems to have been dependent upon Chinese versions that were themselves abridgments and to have extracted a narrative line that does not always make good logical sense. Further on, the problem is that the *Konjaku* compiler is trying to reconcile two (or more) different versions: the episode in which Nanda sees the beautiful monkey-woman must be a conflation of one in which Nanda is taken to see a revoltingly hideous monkey-woman with the episode in which he is shown divine women whose beauty makes him forget his wife. The episode of the hideous monkey-woman is common to a number of Chinese and Indic texts of the story while quite lacking in others. There were evidently diverging traditions about Nanda among the various Buddhist schools in India. Probably the fullest version of the tale is the narrative poem Saundarānanda by the first century A.D. poet Aśvaghoṣa (this poem and his Buddhacarita are the two earliest examples of Sanskrit mahākāvya). It is logically coherent (the reason the Buddha goes away hungry from Nanda's house is that Nanda is engaged in love-play with his wife and oblivious that he has a caller; then, from a high window, he sees the Buddha depart and hurries after him) and emphasizes the fact, mentioned in a later story in *Konjaku* but overlooked in this one, that handsome Nanda was the Buddha's younger brother. Nevertheless, it lacks the supernatural exuberance of the *Konjaku* version: Nanda's final conversion takes place because of a harangue by Ānanda, not a visit to hell. There is a translation by E. H. Johnston, *The Saundarananda: or Nanda the Fair* (London: Oxford University Press, 1932).

2. The same motif of a building with doors that magically open and close in such a way as to prevent someone from entering or exiting appears in one of the stories in the Japanese portion (24:5); there the point is simply the skill of the builder. A translation is included in Frank, pp. 158–160.

Chapter Two

1. ABOUT THE DEATH OF THE BUDDHA'S FATHER, KING ŚUDDHODANA

AT A TIME NOW PAST, when the Buddha's father, King Śuddhodana of Kapilavastu, had become old, he contracted an illness. For several days he suffered with the utmost severity. The pain was so intense that it was as though oil were being squeezed from his body. Soon he would die, he thought; and he grieved that he would die without seeing his son the Buddha Śākyamuni, Nanda, his grandson Rāhula, or his nephew Ānanda.

He sent to inform the Buddha, but the Buddha at that time was in the country of Śrāvastī, fifty yojanas from Kapilavastu. Surely the King would die while the messenger was on the way. The queen and ministers were filled with anxiety; but meanwhile the Buddha, on the Vulture Peak, knew without being told that the King was ill and the people were all lamenting. Leading Nanda, Ānanda, and Rāhula, he went to King Śuddhodana's palace. As he did so, a golden light suddenly illuminated every corner and crevice of the palace, as though the light of morning were shining in.

The astonishment of the King, and of the multitude after him, was unbounded. When the light shone upon the King, all the pain of illness suddenly went away, and he experienced limitless ease. After a little while the Buddha came down from the sky, leading Nanda, Ānanda, and Rāhula. From the moment he saw him, the King's tears fell like rain; he joined his palms in reverence and rejoiced. Standing by his father's side, the Buddha expounded a sutra of cause and effect, and the King immediately attained the fruits of never-returning. The King took the Buddha's hand and drew it to his breast, and thereupon attained the fruits of arhatship.[1] Not long afterwards, the King's life came to an end.

All within the city, whether of high or of low degree, cried out until the city resounded with their lamentations. Immediately, a coffin was made of the seven precious substances, and the King's body was bathed in perfumed water, dressed in brocade, and laid within it. When he died, the Buddha and Nanda were at his pillow, and Ānanda and Rāhula were at his feet. And now at the time of his father's obsequies, the Buddha shouldered his father's coffin, in order to admonish sentient beings in our own latter age against ingratitude for our fathers' and mothers' loving care. As he did so, there was a great earthquake. The earth trembled, and all the different sorts of living beings suddenly bobbed about tumultuously, as when boats encounter waves in the sea.

Thereupon the Four Deva Kings begged the Buddha that they might take his father's coffin on their shoulders. The Buddha gave them leave and himself took up a censer and walked in front of the King. The burial place was on top of the Vulture Peak. As they were about to ascend, arhats came and gathered sandalwood that had been washed up on the shores of the sea and cremated the King's body. The heavens resounded. The Buddha preached the Gātha on Impermanence.[2] When the cremation was finished, the relics were gathered up. These were placed in a golden casket, and the people erected a stupa over it. So the tale's been told, and so it's been handed down.

Notes to Story 1

1. Never-returning and arhatship are the third and fourth of the "four fruits," grades of attainment of those who have entered upon the Buddha path. The never-returner will be reborn not in this world but in the heavens and will thereafter attain nirvana. For the arhat, see 1:11, note 3.

2. A brief verse, beginning with the words "all phenomena are impermanent," which appears in the fourteenth chapter of Dharmarakṣa's translation of the Mahāparinirvāṇa sutra.

21. HOW A GOD HEARD THE DHARMA AND OBTAINED THE CLEAR VISION OF THE DHARMA EYE

AT A TIME NOW PAST, when the Buddha was residing in Jetavana,[1] a god came down from the sky. Seeing this heavenly being, the Buddha preached the Dharma of the Four Truths. By hearing this Dharma the god immediately obtained the clear vision of the Dharma eye.

Ānanda then said to the Buddha, "What brought it about that you have preached the Four Truths to this god and caused him to obtain the Dharma eye?" The Buddha said, "When Master Sudatta built this retreat, he had a slave sweep the garden and tidy up the path. Through the roots of good karma thus established, the slave, when he died, was reborn in the Trayastriṁśa heaven. This god was that slave. It is for that cause that he has come down and seen me, heard the Dharma, and obtained the clear vision of the Dharma eye."

Such was the merit of sweeping the temple garden, even though it was in obedience to another's words and not because of the sweeper's own faith. You may imagine what then would be the merit of one who swept the garden in single-minded devotion! So the tale's been told, and so it's been handed down.

Note to Story 21

1. A park near Śrāvastī given the Buddha by a wealthy man named Sudatta.

Chapter Three

14. ABOUT KING PRASENAJIT'S DAUGHTER UGLY ADAMANTINA

AT A TIME NOW PAST, in the kingdom of Śrāvastī in India, there was a king called Prasenajit. His queen, whose name was Mallikā, was in every way so beautiful that she had no peer in any of the sixteen great kingdoms of India. She gave birth to a daughter whose skin was like that of a poisonous snake. Its stench was such that no one could come near her, and she had wiry hair that curled to the left just like a demon's. In all, she scarcely resembled a human being. Only the King, the Queen, and a wet-nurse had knowledge of her appearance, and everyone else was kept in ignorance of it. The King said to the Queen, "This child of yours is Ugly Adamantina. She is utterly horrible. She must be taken to live in a place apart." A hut ten feet square was built half a mile north of the palace, and she was made to live there in confinement. The wet-nurse and a single maid were her only companions, and no one was allowed in or out.

When Ugly Adamantina reached her twelfth or thirteenth year, each of the kings of the sixteen kingdoms of India, surmising from her mother's flawless beauty that she too must be beautiful, sought to make her his queen. But her father the King refused them all. He took an ordinary man and made him a minister on the spot, and declaring that this should be the bridegroom, espoused him to his ugly daughter. Day and night this "minister" bewailed the dreadfulness of his lot; but he went to live in her house, for he could not disobey the King's command.

Now the King, in fulfillment of a lifetime vow, with pious zeal convoked an assembly to hear the Dharma. Ugly Adamantina was his eldest daughter, but since she was so ugly, she did not attend the assembly. None of the other ministers had any idea what she looked like, and they became suspicious because she did not attend. They plotted to make the King's son-in-law drink wine, and when he was well in his cups they stole the key he carried at his waist and sent an under-official to his house to find out for them what his wife looked like. Now, before the messenger's arrival, Ugly Adamantina had been sitting alone in her house, in sorrow: "O Śākyamuni Buddha, I pray you, change me and make me beautiful; bring it about that I may attend my father's Dharma assembly." Just then the Buddha appeared within her courtyard. When Ugly Adamantina saw the Buddha's countenance, she was filled with joy, and on account of her joy the beauty of the Buddha himself was imprinted upon her person. She thought that she would announce the transformation to her husband at once; but meanwhile the under-official stole up to her house and gazed in through a crack. Within he saw a woman as flawlessly beautiful as the Buddha. He returned to the ministers and reported: "Such loveliness I could not even imagine. Never in all my life have I seen a woman so beautiful."

The King's son-in-law awoke and went to his house, where he saw a beautiful woman whom he did not recognize. Not daring to approach, he asked her mistrustfully, "Who are you who have deigned to come to my house?" "I am your wife, Adamantina," the woman said. "That cannot be," the husband said. The woman said, "I must hasten to join my father's Dharma assembly. It is because I have received Śākyamuni's own welcome that I am altered into her whom you see before you." Hearing this, the minister ran back to the King to report it. In the palace the King and Queen listened in astonishment and immediately had their palanquins taken to her house so they could see for themselves. So beautiful was she that there was nothing in this world to which she could be compared. They greeted her at once as their daughter and brought her into the palace.

When she had joined in the Dharma assembly, as she had prayed to do, the King accompanied his daughter into the Buddha's presence and inquired minutely into what had taken place. "Listen well," said the Buddha. "In a former life this woman was a kitchen maid in your house. A certain holy man used to come to your house to receive alms. With meritorious resolve, you had set aside a bag of rice so that all members of your household, whether of high or low degree, could make offerings from it to the monk with their own hands. This maid, among all your servants, abused the monk for his ugliness even as she was making the offering. The monk thereupon came before you, O King, and revealing his divinity, ascended into the sky and entered nirvana.

When the woman saw this she wept aloud, repenting the sin of abusing him. Because of her offerings to the monk, she has now been born as the daughter of a great king; but because of the sin of abusing a monk, it was with the face and form of a demon. But because she awakened to her fault and repented of it, today she has heard my preaching; her demon's shape was altered into flawless beauty, and she has entered the Buddha path forever. For this reason, never abuse a monk. And if you should commit sins, you must repent them with all your heart. Repentance is the first means of establishing the roots of good karma." This the Buddha taught. So the tale's been told, and so it's been handed down.

28. WHAT THE BUDDHA SAID TO THE SANGHA WHEN HE WAS ABOUT TO ENTER NIRVANA

AT A TIME NOW PAST, Śākyamuni Tathāgata for over forty years preached the many different sorts of Dharma to benefit all sentient beings both in the heavens and in the human world and had reached the age of eighty. While in the country of Vaiśālī he said to Ānanda, "Now I suffer in all my limbs; within three months I shall enter nirvana." Ānanda said to the Buddha, "You have already escaped all illness. Why do you now suffer?" The Buddha thereupon arose; sending forth a great light which illuminated the world, he seated himself in the posture for meditation. All the beings whom this light shone upon felt comfort and were freed from pain.

From Vaiśālī he went to Kuśinagara; between twin trees in a grove of teak trees he lay like a lion[1] on his bed. He said to Ānanda, "You must know that soon I will enter nirvana. Whatever flourishes must decay; whatever is born is destined to die." And to Mañjuśrī[2] he said, "I shall explain for the benefit of the sangha[3] why my back pains me. Never being ill results from two conditions. The first of these is compassion for sentient beings, and the second is giving medicine to the sick. For incalculable kalpas I have practiced the way of the bodhisattva; always I have benefited living beings and freed them from distress, and I have given all the different sorts of medicines to the sick. Why then should I experience illness? Because once, long ago, I struck a deer upon its back, and as I now approach nirvana the karmic fruits of that deed are manifested."

Mahākāśyapa summoned the physician Jīva and inquired about the marks of the Buddha's condition. Jīva said, "The Buddha will shortly enter nirvana. No medicine will avail." Mahākāśyapa and the other members of the sangha sorrowed boundlessly upon hearing the physician's words. It need scarcely be said that Jīva also sorrowed as they did.

But who among men or gods, among all the sangha, would not have sorrowed upon seeing that the Buddha was about to enter nirvana? So the tale's been told, and so it's been handed down.

Notes to Story 28

1. This denotes a specific posture, probably familiar to many readers from sculptural representations of the parinirvāṇa: lying on the right side, the head supported on the right elbow, the legs straight.

2. Mañjuśrī (Japanese, Monju) is the bodhisattva who exemplifies wisdom; he is often depicted standing on the left side of Śākyamuni. In accounts of the life of the Buddha such as the present one there is a continuum among human, semidivine, and divine actors.

3. The sangha is the congregation of believers: monks and nuns, pious laymen and pious laywomen.

Chapter Four

9. HOW BODHIDHARMA OF INDIA WENT TO THIS PLACE AND THAT OBSERVING THE DEVOTIONS OF THE MONKS

AT A TIME NOW PAST, in India, there was a holy man called the Venerable Bodhidharma. He traveled through all of India, carefully examined the religious practices of the different sorts of monks, and taught them to the world.

There was a certain temple which he entered to observe the ways of the monks. A great many monks resided there. In some of the chambers they were offering flowers and incense before the Buddha; in others, they were chanting the scriptures. In their different ways, all monks alike were engaged in the most worthy activities. There was one house, however, which looked entirely uninhabited. It was dirty and surrounded by tall weeds. Bodhidharma went inside. At the rear of the chamber he saw two monks in their eighties who were sitting and playing go. No image of the Buddha was to be seen, nor were there any sacred books. To all appearances, the sole occupation of the two old men was playing go. Bodhidharma went out and met a monk. "I went into such-and-such a cell," he said, "where there was nothing but two old men sitting and playing go." "Those two old men," said the monk, "from their earliest youth have done nothing but play go. They scarcely know that such a thing as the Buddha's teaching exists. The other monks don't like them and won't have anything to do with them. For years those idlers have eaten food and done nothing for it, for all their time is spent on go. They might as well be heathens. Don't even get near them."

Bodhidharma thought, "Those two men must have a reason for acting as they do," and he went back to the cell where they were playing go. He sat beside them and watched. Whenever one had set a piece down, he would stand up, while the one whose turn it was remained sitting. After a little while, the one who was sitting vanished as though into thin air. Just as Bodhidharma was thinking how strange it was, there they were again, the two of them.

Again one vanished; and again after a little while he reappeared. Bodhidharma was astounded. He thought, "The other monks despise these two and shun them because all they do is play go, but that is a grievous error. In reality these are two holy men of exalted worth. Let me ask them about their behavior."

The Venerable Bodhidharma questioned the two old men: "How can this be? When I heard that you had passed years and months with go as your sole occupation I observed you carefully and found that you are indeed men who have attained the fruits of enlightenment.[1] Explain it to me."

The two old men replied, "For years now we have done nothing but play go. But we consider that whenever black wins, the passions wax within our bodies, and when white wins, bodhi grows within our hearts, and that the white of bodhi subdues the black of passion. We use the occasion to contemplate Impermanence.[2] The merits of this practice have borne present reward, and we have gained the fruits of enlightenment." When Bodhidharma heard this, his tears fell like rain and his remorse was boundless. He said, "In this manner you have for years concealed your devotions and your religious merit; you let no one have the least inkling of them and made the people in the temple think you idle and shameless. Here are noble minds indeed!" and doing homage to them over and over again, he went out of the chamber. He met some other monks, to whom he told the story. All the monks heard about it and were filled with reverence. They bitterly regretted their stupidity: for years they had scorned enlightened arhats through failing to recognize them.

His Reverence Bodhidharma left the temple and went to a village at the foot of the mountains, where he spent the night. In the night he heard a voice shouting: "A gang of robbers is here and they're going to kill me. The treasure I've been guarding for many years has all been stolen. People of the village, save me!" At the cry, the villagers all appeared with lighted torches. "Where does the voice come from?" they said. One man said, "It's from the house of that holy man in the eastern grove! Let's take a look over there." The villagers seized bows and arrows and rushed off, torches in their hands. "The holy man says he's being killed. What's going on?" His Reverence Bodhidharma went with them. In the midst of a grove there was a grass hut no larger than a big umbrella, with a door of plaited brushwood. When they pulled it

open, Bodhidharma saw sitting within a monk in his eighties.
The monk wore only a patchwork stole and had nothing before
him but an armrest. In all the hut there was nothing for a thief to
take; nor was there any thief. When he saw the people coming,
the holy man wept without restraint.

The villagers questioned the holy man. "We can see nothing in
your chamber for a thief to take. What on earth made you shout
like that?" The holy man replied, "Well you may ask! Sleep, that
thief who for years had never so much as entered my chamber,
came in at twilight tonight to rob me of the treasure of seven
sacred graces laid up in my mind's storehouse, and lest they be
taken from me I wrestled with him shouting," and he wept without restraint. The Venerable Bodhidharma thought, "Ordinary
people just stretch out and go to sleep, but this holy man has not
slept for years, and when by chance he starts to go to sleep he
makes an outcry of this sort." Bodhidharma swore an oath of
discipleship with him and then went home, as did the villagers.

The Venerable Bodhidharma went to yet another village, and
there he saw a monk all by himself in a grove. The moment that
man started to sit, he stood up. The moment he started to stand,
he ran. The moment he started to run, he went around and
around. The moment he started to turn around, he lay down. The
moment he started to lie down he stood up. He faced east; he faced
south; he faced west; he faced north. The moment he laughed, he
got angry; the moment he got angry, he cried. Anyone who saw
him would think he was crazy. Bodhidharma went up to him and
asked, "Why do you act this way, sir?" The crazy monk replied,
"Such is the nature of man that no sooner is he born in heaven
than he is reborn as a human being; no sooner is he reborn among
men than he drops into hell. No sooner does he drop into hell
than he falls into the realm of the hungry ghosts; no sooner does
he fall into the realm of the hungry ghosts than he becomes an
asura.[3] No sooner does he become an asura than he is born among
the beasts. Now, the inquietude of the Three Worlds[4] is like that
of my conduct. For years I have gone about as a madman in the
hope that when men of understanding see the ugliness of what I
do they will recognize the mutability of the Three Worlds."
Hearing him, Bodhidharma knew that here was no ordinary man
and before departing did homage to him.

Such was the manner in which the Venerable Bodhidharma

traveled and observed the practices of the worthy monks. So the tale's been told, and so it's been handed down.

Notes to Story 9

1. Spiritual attainment confers magical powers, such as clairvoyance and the ability to disappear at will.

2. Bodhidharma is known in the West as the bringer of Zen from India to China, so that it might be worth reminding the reader that *Konjaku* was compiled a good many years prior to the formal introduction of Zen to Japan in 1191; the story of Bodhidharma and the two monks who play go can in fact be found as early as 668, in a Chinese collection of exempla, *Fa-yüan chu-lin,* compiled by the monk Tao-shih. It appears also in *Uji shūi monogatari,* a *setsuwa* collection compiled ca. 1213–1219 (see Mills, p. 355, for a translation), and there the monks attain enlightenment simply by pitting white against black—precisely the sort of quizzical behavior one might expect in an anecdote about Zen. But by having the monks explain that they make their game the occasion to contemplate Impermanence, the *Konjaku* compiler, like Tao-shih before him, shows that what he is serving up is actually standard Buddhist doctrinal fare, however strikingly illustrated. The two episodes that follow are likewise striking illustrations of standard Buddhist teachings; their point, unlike that of Zen kōan, is not the irrationality or suprarationality of truth, but that apparently bizarre behavior can have an eminently rational explanation. Such a point is just what one would expect the *Konjaku* compiler to make, and it may be significant that these two episodes are preserved in this text alone.

3. A kind of demonic being; see 4:34, note 1.

4. Of past, present, and future.

24. HOW NĀGĀRJUNA, WHILE A LAYMAN, MADE A CHARM FOR INVISIBILITY

AT A TIME NOW PAST, in western[1] India, there was a holy man whom people called the Bodhisattva Nāgārjuna. While still a layman he had studied the formulae in the canons of the heathens. At that time there were three such laymen. They consulted together and prepared a medicine that conferred invisibility. To make this medicine, you cut a piece of mistletoe five inches long and dry it in the shade for a hundred days;[2] it's that sort of medicine. Once you've mastered the formula, when you wear the stem in your topknot it's just as though you had on that cloak of invisibility one hears of. Nobody will see you.

Now these three men did just as they pleased: they stuck charms for invisibility into their hair and went into the King's palace and violated the royal ladies. The ladies were terrified at the touch of beings whom they could not see and complained in private to the King. "In recent days invisible beings have come to molest us," they said. The King listened, and being astute, he thought, "Whoever did this must have made the medicine of invisibility. It can be nothing else. The way to deal with it is to sprinkle powder everywhere throughout the palace. Even though the person's body is invisible, he will leave footprints that show where he goes." This was his scheme. He ordered great quantities of powder to be sprinkled everywhere throughout the palace. By "powder" is meant rice powder. Powder was strewn thickly everywhere, so that when these three men were inside the palace their footprints became evident, whereupon the King sent in a lot of swordsmen with weapons drawn. The swordsmen guessed where the men were from their tracks, and two of the men were cut down. Only one man remained. It was the Bodhisattva Nāgārjuna. Despairing for his life, he pulled the hem of a royal lady's skirt over his head and lay there. Many virtuous resolves arose in his heart. It must have been in token of these good resolves that, after the other two had been cut down, the King said, "These then are the invisible beings. So there were two!" The pursuit was ended. Nāgārjuna waited for a moment when the people were off their guard, slipped away, and fled the palace. Afterwards, in the realization that the heathen arts were profitless, he renounced secular life at——. He practiced and taught the Dharma of the Buddha; it is he whom we call the Bodhisattva Nāgārjuna. The whole world honors him and accords him boundless reverence. So the tale's been told, and so it's been handed down.

Notes to Story 24

1. Evidently a copyist's error for southern.

2. A variant text of *Konjaku* says that the mistletoe should be three inches long and it should be dried for three hundred days.

34. HOW TWO BROTHERS, MEN OF INDIA, CARRIED GOLD THROUGH THE MOUNTAINS

AT A TIME NOW PAST, there were in India two brothers who went on a journey together, each carrying a thousand taels of gold. As they made their way through the mountains, the elder thought, "If I were to kill my brother and steal his thousand taels of gold, with the thousand I already have I would have two thousand taels of gold." The younger also thought, "If I were to kill my brother and steal his thousand taels of gold, with the thousand I already have I would have two thousand taels of gold. How I should like that!"

Each thought the same thing about the other, but before either could resolve on the deed, they had passed through the mountains and come out upon the banks of a river. The elder brother threw the thousand taels of gold he was carrying into the river. The younger brother saw this and asked, "Why did you throw the gold into the river?" The elder replied, "As we were passing through the mountains I felt an urge to kill you and take your gold. You are the only brother I have; would I have wanted to kill you were it not for this gold? Therefore I have cast it away." The younger brother said, "In just the same way I too wanted to kill you. It is all the fault of the gold," and he too threw the gold that he had been carrying into the river.

People are robbed of their lives because of the cravings of the senses and incur bodily harm because of worldly goods. He who possesses none and remains poor will have no cause for grief. And indeed, it is the craving for worldly goods that causes us to wander among the Six Paths of Transmigration and the Four Kinds of Birth.[1] So the tale's been told, and so it's been handed down.

Note to Story 34

1. The Six Paths are the six levels of reincarnation: in hell, as a hungry ghost, as an animal, as an asura, as a human being, as a god; see the final episode in 4:9. The Four Kinds of Birth are from the womb, from the egg, from moisture, and by transformation.

41. HOW A MAN FOR LOVE OF HIS CHILD
WENT TO KING YAMA'S PALACE

AT A TIME NOW PAST, there was in India a bhikshu who practiced religion in the hope that he might become an arhat. He
reached the age of sixty, but he was unable to become an arhat:
much as it grieved him his powers simply did not suffice. The
man therefore returned to his home. "For years I have practiced
religion in the hope of becoming an arhat," he thought, "but I
have not achieved my goal. Let me now return to lay life and live
as a householder," and he became a layman again. He took a wife,
and this wife soon became pregnant and bore a beautiful boy on
whom the father lavished boundless love. When the boy reached
his seventh year, quite unexpectedly he died. In his grief the
father refused to have the body taken away. When his neighbors
heard of this they came to him and said, "You are foolish in the
extreme. To refuse to let the body of a dead child be taken away
because you grieve for him is extraordinarily foolish. Even if it is
not taken away, you cannot preserve it forever. It must be disposed of immediately," and they took it away from him by force.

   The father could not bear his sorrow, and he vowed that he
would see his son again. "I shall go to King Yama[1] and ask to see
my child," he thought. He did not know where King Yama was to
be found, and as he was seeking him he met a man who said, "Go
in such-and-such a direction for thus-and-so a distance, and you
will find King Yama's palace and a great river. On the banks of
that river is a palace formed of the seven precious substances.
King Yama is within."

   The father continued his search as he was instructed, hasten-
ing onward and ever onward until he did in truth espy a great
river. On the riverbank stood a palace formed of the seven precious substances. Trembling with fear in the midst of his rejoicing, he drew near. A man of exalted station and noble bearing
questioned him: "Who are you?" "I am so-and-so," he replied.
"My son died in his seventh year. I could not bear my longing for
him, and I have come to ask the King to let me see him. I pray
you, O King, because you are merciful, show me my child!" The
King replied, "I shall show you your child at once. He is in the
rear garden. Go and look." Overjoyed, the father went where he

was told. There he saw his child: he was playing with some other little boys like himself.

The father called the boy to him and took him by the hand, and said, weeping, "I have longed for you so much in recent days that I have asked the King to be allowed to see you. Haven't you missed me as much as I've missed you?" Tears streamed down his face as he spoke, but the boy did not seem at all sad; not thinking of him as his father, he ran back to play. The father wept in endless, bitter grief. The boy, however, did not even wonder why and said nothing. The father's lamentations were useless, and he returned home.

Once one has parted from a life one no longer has the same feelings, so it appears. Wasn't it because the father was still in the same life that he felt such longing for his boy? So the tale's been told, and so it's been handed down.

Note to Story 41

1. King Yama (Japanese, Enma-ō) rules over the world of the dead, judging sinners and sentencing them to hell (or rather, the hells, as these are multiple). Although his helpers are pictured as demons whose task, as in the story of Nanda, is to torture sinners, he himself is envisioned as a just, wise, and pious magistrate.

Chapter Five

2. HOW A KING WENT INTO THE MOUNTAINS TO HUNT DEER AND WAS ROBBED OF HIS DAUGHTER BY A LION

AT A TIME NOW PAST, there was in India a kingdom whose King made a progress into the mountains. He sent men into the valleys and up to the peaks; blowing conches and beating drums, they started the deer from their cover for the King's sport. The King had a daughter whom he loved tenderly, and since he never allowed her from his side even for an instant, he had her accompany him in a palanquin.

As the afternoon drew on, the beaters who had gone into the mountains in pursuit of deer entered a cave where a lion was sleeping. They aroused not deer but the lion, who awoke with a start and went out onto the mountainside roaring in a majestic and terrifying voice. The men all fled in panic; many of them fell to the ground as they ran. The men who had borne the princess's palanquin abandoned it and took to their heels. The King, too, fled, in such consternation that he scarcely knew east from west, and returned to his palace. When he inquired about the princess's palanquin, it was reported to him that the bearers had all left it in the mountains and fled. Hearing this, the King fell into a frenzy of weeping. She must not remain there, and he despatched many men to the mountains, but so fearful were they that none dared go near.

Driven from his lair, the lion pawed the ground and roared in rage. As he coursed the mountains he saw a palanquin. He ripped away the hangings with his teeth and saw seated inside it a woman bright as a jewel. Gleefully he set her upon his back and took her to the cave in which he had been dwelling and embraced her carnally. The princess lay totally unconscious, in a state that was neither life nor death.

The lion cohabited with the princess for many years. She became pregnant; her months were fulfilled and she gave birth to a child. The child was a normal human being, a boy, beautiful as

can be. When he had passed his tenth year he was braver and
fleeter of foot than others. From his mother's face he knew that
she spent her days in sorrow. While the lion his father was out
seeking food he asked her, "Mother, why do you always look sad
and weep? Is something troubling you? There is a bond between
parent and child; do not conceal your sorrow from me." The
mother wept all the more and for a long while said nothing. At
length she spoke amidst her tears. "I am in fact the daughter of
the King of this country." And then she recounted everything
that had taken place, from the beginning to that very day. Hearing her tale, he too wept without restraint. He said to his mother,
"If you want to go to the capital I shall take you there before
father comes. I know just how fast my father can run, and though
he is as fast as I am, he cannot outrun me. I will take you to the
capital and hide you and take care of you. Even though I am the
son of a lion, I am closer to my mother's line, for I was born a man.
I shall take you to the capital at once. Hurry, get on my back."
And the mother, to her joy, was put on her son's back.

Once he had his mother on his back he went to the capital,
swift as a bird can fly. From kindly persons he obtained lodgings
where he installed his mother in secret and attended assiduously
to her needs. When the lion returned to his cave he saw neither
wife nor child and realized that they had fled to the capital.
Loving them, longing for them, he went toward the capital, roaring his agitation. The people of the country heard him, and all,
the King not excepted, were scared out of their wits. Upon due
consideration, the King issued a decree: "Be it known that whoever kills the lion and puts an end to his depredations will be
given half of my kingdom."

The lion's son heard the decree and said to the King, "If I kill
the lion and bring you his head, will you reward me?" "Kill him
and bring me his head," said the King. Hearing the King's command, the lion's son thought, "To kill a father is the worst of
crimes, but if I become king of half a kingdom I can do my duty
by my mother, and she is a human being." Bow and arrows in
hand, he went to the place where his father was. When the lion
saw his son, he rolled about on the ground in ecstasy. He lay on
his back and stretched out his paws, licking his child's head and
caressing him — whereupon the son shot a poisoned arrow into
the lion's side. The lion so loved his son that he showed not the

slightest sign of anger but licked his child's head all the harder
even as the tears gushed from his eyes. After a short time he died.
The child then cut off his father's head, carried it back to the
capital, and presented it at once to the King. The King viewed it
in horror. As he prepared to divide his kingdom, he first inquired
about the circumstances of the slaying. The lion's son thought
that now was the occasion to explain the reason behind it and to
reveal that he was the King's grandson. He therefore told the
King, just as his mother had told him, all that had happened, from
the beginning to that very day.

"So this is my grandson!" the King thought. He was supposed
to divide his kingdom as he had originally decreed; but he said to
himself, "If I reward a man who has killed his father, I will share
in his crime, and if I do not give him his reward, I will be false to
my promise. I must therefore give him a country apart." He
bestowed a country on him and sent mother as well as child there.
The lion's son lived in that country as its king. His throne was
inherited by sons and grandsons who reside there even now.
Indeed, the name of that country is "Seize-the-Lion country."[1] So
the tale's been told, and so it's been handed down.

Note to Story 2

1. Siṁhala (*siṁha,* lion). The story immediately preceding this in *Konjaku* explains the name instead as that of the merchant who settled in
the island after outwitting its prior inhabitants, a throng of female
demons of the kind called rakshasis. (A version of the story of the
merchant appears in *Uji shūi monogatari,* translated in Mills, pp. 266–
269.)

13. HOW THE THREE BEASTS PRACTICED
THE WAY OF THE BODHISATTVA
AND THE RABBIT ROASTED HIMSELF

AT A TIME NOW PAST, in India, there were three beasts, a rabbit,
a fox, and a monkey. In all three sincere aspiration for enlightenment had been aroused, so that they practiced the way of the

bodhisattva. Each one thought, "It is because of the sinfulness of our former lives that we have been reborn as lowly beasts. In our former lives we lacked charity toward living beings. We hoarded our worldly goods and gave nothing to others. So deep were our sins that we fell into hell and endured prolonged torment and then, through the karma that yet remained, were reborn as animals. In this life, however, let us sacrifice ourselves." Those far advanced in years, they honored as parents; those a little their senior, they treated as older brothers; those a little younger, they treated tenderly as younger brothers. They abandoned selfish concerns and put the welfare of others first.

The god Indra saw this and thought, "Though their bodies are those of beasts, their minds are noble. Of the beings that are born as men, some kill living creatures, some steal other men's goods, some kill father or mother, some regard their brothers as deadly enemies, some disguise evil thoughts with smiles or harbor rage behind loving countenances, How much more difficult then to believe that animals such as these sincerely aspire to enlightenment! I shall test them." He forthwith assumed the appearance of a man far gone in years, weak, spent, and helpless, and went to where the three beasts were staying. He said, "I am old and feeble and unable to care for myself. You there, you three beasts, feed me. I have no children; my household is poor and I have nothing to eat. I have heard that you three beasts are deeply compassionate." Hearing him, the three beasts said, "This is exactly what we had intended from the first. He must be fed immediately." The monkey climbed trees and brought back chestnuts, persimmons, pears, jujubes, tangerines, oranges, gooseberries, hazelnuts, vine-plums, and akebia fruit;[1] he went out into the fields and brought back cucumbers, eggplants, soybeans, red beans, cowpeas, and three kinds of millet and had the old man eat whatever he liked. The fox went to a neighborhood where there were funeral sheds and brought back plain and fancy rice-cakes, abalone, and bonito and other sorts of fish which people had left there as offerings and gave the old man whatever he thought would suit his taste, until he was sated.

Thus several days passed. The old man said, "These two beasts truly have profound aspirations. They are fully bodhisattvas." Meanwhile the rabbit, filled with eager striving, took a torch, took incense, pricked his ears up and arched his back, widened

his eyes and flexed his forelegs and opened the gap in his hindquarters, scampering north, south, east, west in search of food but
obtained nothing at all. And so, the monkey and the fox and the
old man on the one hand shamed him and on the other hand
laughed him to scorn; they egged him on, but his powers did not
suffice. The rabbit thought, "I might go to the fields and mountains to look for food, but the fields and mountains are full of
danger. I would be killed by men or devoured by beasts. I would
only be wasting my life. It would be far better if I were now to
sacrifice my body, be eaten by this old man, and depart this
present birth forever." He went to the old man and said, "Now I
am going out to look for delicacies. While you wait, please gather
wood and light a fire." And so the monkey gathered wood and the
fox brought fire and lit the wood, and they waited to see if the
rabbit might possibly bring anything. The rabbit brought nothing. When the monkey and the fox saw him, they said, "We
wondered what you would bring. It was just as we thought all
along! You lied to us and fooled us into making a fire so you could
warm yourself. How disgusting!" The rabbit said, "I haven't the
power to find food and bring it back. But I will roast my own body
for him to eat," and he leaped into the fire and was burned to
death.

Then the god Indra resumed his original form and transferred
to the moon the shape of the rabbit in the fire. He put this image
on the moon to show to all sentient beings everywhere. And so,
what looks like a cloud on the surface of the moon is the smoke
from the fire in which the rabbit was roasting. And when people
talk about the rabbit in the moon they mean this image of a
rabbit. You myriad folk, whenever you look at the moon, you
should think of the story of this rabbit.[2]

<hr>

Notes to Story 13

<hr>

1. I have omitted from this list one item, which seemed to be
redundant.

2. The usual closing formula is lacking here.

Tales of China

Accounts of visits to the afterworld were a staple of Buddhist preaching, as were stories intended to demonstrate the merit of such practices as copying and chanting the sutras and praising the Buddhas. Such motifs appear throughout *Konjaku,* sometimes in complex settings; in Chapters Six and Seven they are presented almost unadorned. Chapter Eight is missing. A large part of Chapter Nine is concerned with Confucian morality, and the stories translated from this chapter all illustrate the principles of filial piety, though in rather different ways. Chapter Ten is devoted to secular history and begins, appropriately enough, with a capsule history of China's First Emperor and his short-lived dynasty. The story of Wu Chao-hsiao combines two well-loved Chinese sentimental themes: that of the lonely, cloistered existence led by the emperor's supernumerary concubines as they wait in vain to be noticed by their master, and that of lovers unknowingly destined for each other. The two stories of Chuang Tzu are typical of the affectionate anecdotes told in Japan about the Chinese mystic philosopher.

Chapter Six

34. HOW A NOVICE OF THE K'UNG-KUAN SSU IN CHINA VIEWED THE LOTUS-MATRIX WORLD AND RETURNED TO LIFE

AT A TIME NOW PAST, in a temple in China called K'ung-kuan ssu, there was a novice monk whose name was Ting-sheng. Monk though he was, he broke the ordinances of the sangha, and not once did he recite the holy teachings.

Now, one of the monks preached a sermon that described the Lotus-Matrix World.[1] Ting-sheng heard it with joy and constantly and fervently prayed to be reborn there. But he went on breaking the rules for monks just as he pleased; and in the end he died and fell into the Red Lotus Hell.[2] When Ting-sheng saw this hell he thought it was the Lotus-Matrix World and, rapt in contemplation, exclaimed: "Homage to the Lotus-Matrix World!" No sooner had he spoken than the hell was transformed: it became indeed the Lotus-Matrix World. Moreover, all the sinners who heard Ting-sheng lift his voice in praise of the Lotus-Matrix World were now seated upon lotus flowers. The demonic tormentors who witnessed this marvel reported it to King Yama. Yama said, "This has come about through the miraculous power of the Wreath Sutra," and thereupon recited this gāthā:

> We trust in the Wreath, the sutra of marvels;
> If a man speaks its name, speaks one four-word verse,
> He can destroy the hells, cast off karmic fetters:
> All the hells become ——— [3]

The novice monk saw that the hell had become a lotus-matrix and that every one of the sinners in it was now seated on a lotus flower. After a day and a night he returned to life and recounted what had occurred. Afterwards he attained enlightened understanding; faith was aroused in his heart and he cultivated virtue. What happened to him later on, no one knows. So the tale's been told, and so it's been handed down.

Notes to Story 34

1. A Pureland paradise established by the Buddha Vairocana in the blossom of a lotus that grows out of the perfumed sea above the wheel of the winds surrounding the earth. It is described in the Wreath Sutra (a somewhat different description appears in the Brahma's Net Sutra). Rebirth in a paradise was to be followed by direct attainment of nirvana. In 10:32 a dying monk declares that a heavenly messenger has arrived to take him to the Tuṣita heaven but that he prefers to wait for rebirth in the Lotus-Matrix World. Despite the popularity of the Pureland concept in Japan, references in literature to Vairocana's paradise are rare aside from these two stories: the Pureland that became the focus of popular religious practice was that established by Amitabha in the West. See 1:11, note 2.

2. In Buddhism there are cold as well as hot hells. The Red Lotus Hell was so named because of the appearance of the wounds of the sinners being tortured there, which froze and cracked open.

3. The poem is incomplete in the original. Almost certainly "Purelands" can be supplied at the end of it.

35. HOW SUN HSÜAN-TE COPIED THE WREATH SUTRA

AT A TIME NOW PAST, in China during the T'ang dynasty, there was a titular official named Sun Hsüan-te. He was a man of I-an District. Through an impulse arising from some karmic cause, Hsüan-te made a vow to copy the Wreath Sutra; but something happened, so that he lost faith and forgot about it. Hsüan-te was by nature inclined to bad deeds, and there was no evil that he did not engage in.

Now, while Hsüan-te was out hunting he fell from his horse. In agony, he stopped breathing and died. After a day he returned to life and tearfully repented his sins. To Ssu-miao[1] he said, "No sooner had I died than three officials of the land of the dead came and drove me before them and brought me before a great castle. I saw King Yama seated among the Ministers of the Five Paths.[2] He upbraided me and said, 'You dolt! You gain your livelihood from wrongdoing. I have summoned you for judgment without delay[3]

because the animals you have killed have lodged complaints
against you.' In the court I saw the animals I had killed — a hundred, a thousand, ten thousand. They addressed the King, all
complaining that I had robbed them of their lives without cause.
As the King heard them he fell into an even greater rage.

"Just then a youth suddenly appeared before the King and
announced his name as Sudhana.[4] At the sight of him the King
respectfully got down from his seat and joined his palms in reverent salutation. The boy said, 'Hsüan-te must be released at once.
He made a vow to copy the Wreath Sutra and has not yet fulfilled
it.' The King said, 'True, Hsüan-te made a vow — but he lost faith
and forgot it entirely. Why should I release him?' The youth said,
'Hsüan-te was not lacking in faith when he made his vow. Why
should the earlier good be ignored for the later evil?' The King
heard this and rejoiced. 'Justly spoken! I shall release Hsüan-te at
once and send him home.' Thereupon the youth showed me the
road back; it is thanks to this that I have succeeded in returning to
life. Marvelous is the merit of the Wreath Sutra!" Weeping copiously, he heartily repented his negligence. He immediately made
a copy of the Wreath Sutra and dedicated it, saying to his friends
and relations, "Now I've copied the Wreath Sutra to the end. I'll
be reborn in the Tuṣita heaven and serve the Merciful Bodhisattva."[5] When at last he died he was in his eighty-sixth year.

Truly the merit of the Wreath Sutra is marvelous. So the tale's
been told, and so it's been handed down.

Notes to Story 35

1. Sun Ssu-miao (601–682) was a Taoist physician who achieved celebrity for a treatise on Indian medicine and was interested in Buddhism; a
description of his medical ideas appears in Kenneth Ch'en, *Buddhism
in China* (Princeton: Princeton University Press, 1964), pp. 482–483.

2. Yama's assistants, who aid him in deciding the destinies of the dead.
The Five Paths are the Six Paths of reincarnation enumerated in 4:34,
note 1, minus that of asura, which seems not to have found a place in
the popular imagination in China and Japan.

3. "For judgment without delay" is a guess at the meaning of an obscure
phrase.

4. Sudhana (Japanese, Zenai *dōshi*) appears in the Wreath Sutra as a
youth who is a disciple of Mañjuśrī. The theme of the supernatural

protector (often, as here, associated with a particular sutra) coming before Yama as advocate for a sinner on trial is a common one in *Konjaku* and in Buddhist homiletic literature in general. Characteristically, the sinner has earned his protector's intervention through a meritorious act so slight that he has forgotten it or through having made a meritorious vow that has yet to be fulfilled.

5. Maitreya.

Chapter Seven

18. HOW A NUN OF HO-TUNG IN CHINA CHANTED THE LOTUS SUTRA AND HOW THE TEXT SHE READ FROM WAS ALTERED

AT A TIME NOW PAST, in a place in China called Ho-tung, there was a nun who was assiduous in her devotions. For years she kept her body pure and constantly recited the Lotus Sutra. Moreover, she had a desire to copy the Lotus Sutra, and she hired someone to copy it for her. She gave the scribe painstaking instructions and paid him far more than his usual wage. To provide him with a place pure enough for his task, she had a house especially constructed. Each time that he went outside he bathed and burned incense before reentering. There was a hole in the wall of the building, into which a bamboo tube had been inserted, and whenever the scribe wanted to exhale she made him exhale through that hole. In this manner the copying was carried out in purity, as the ordinances prescribe, and within eight years all seven rolls[1] were completed. She thereupon dedicated them in sincere faith and, once they were dedicated, reverenced them with heartfelt piety.

Now, in a temple called Lung-men there lived a monk whose name was Fa-tuan. He decided to assemble a congregation at his temple to expound the Lotus Sutra, and he thought that he would borrow the sutra that the nun owned as the text for his lecture. When he tried to borrow it, however, she firmly refused to part with it. Fa-tuan pleaded with her and scolded her until, against her own wishes and judgment, she agreed. Rather than send a messenger, she herself carried the sutra to Lung-men and gave it to Fa-tuan.

Having obtained the sutra, Fa-tuan assembled his congregation in joy and prepared to lecture. When he opened the scrolls he saw nothing but yellow paper, and not a single character. He thought this strange and opened the other scrolls. All seven alike were totally devoid of writing. Astounded, he showed them to the congregation, and everyone in the congregation saw exactly what

Fa-tuan had seen. Fa-tuan and the congregation as well became fearful and ashamed, and they sent the sutra back to the nun. She wept to see it; but though she repented having lent it, her repentance availed nothing.

Thereupon she tearfully sprinkled perfumed water on the sutra box; she bathed; she lifted up the sutra in her hands; she scattered flowers and burned incense and circumambulated a statue for seven days and nights without pause; and she prayed with sincere faith that the sutra might be restored. When she opened the scrolls afterwards, the characters had reappeared and were just as before. When she saw this, she shed many tears and reverently rededicated the sutra.

Now think: didn't the characters disappear because, monk though he was, he was insincere? She was only a nun, and yet she restored the words with her prayers: was it not because of the profoundness of her sincerity? That's what people said at the time. So the tale's been told, and so it's been handed down.

Note to Story 18

1. The complete text is meant here, although the recension most often used is in eight, not seven, rolls.

Chapter Nine

4. HOW SOMEONE IN LU-CHOU
KILLED A NEIGHBOR AND WAS NOT PUNISHED

AT A TIME NOW PAST, in Lu-chou in China, there were two brothers who had the same father and different mothers. The elder lost both father and mother in childhood.[1] His younger brother's mother raised him along with her own son. It is only to be expected that a mother will expend care on the instruction and nurture of her own child; but as for the stepson — he received even better care from his stepmother than from a real mother.

Now, a neighbor got drunk, came to their house, and heaped abuse on the mother. The boys hit him to teach him a lesson; and soon he was dead under their blows. Despite the gravity of the crime, out of consideration for their mother the boys did not flee but remained in the house with the gate open. Policemen came to arrest them and were about to put them to death, when the older brother said, "It is I who have committed the crime. I should be executed at once. My brother is not to blame." Likewise the younger brother said, "My brother had nothing to do with the killing. I am the murderer, and so you must execute me." Each offered to yield up his life in place of the other.

The policemen thought this strange, exceedingly strange, and unable to decide on the spot who was the guilty one, went back to inform the King. The King said, "Call the mother and examine her." The woman came in response to the summons. "Why is it," she was asked, "that each of your children at once offers to die in place of the other, and neither one begrudges his own life." The woman said, "The fault is mine alone. I was the one who taught the boys; I caused them to kill." The King said, "There is a limit to the responsibility for a crime. You cannot take your children's offense upon yourself or suffer their punishment. Both sons ought by rights to be put to death, but I will execute one and pardon the other. Tell me now: which child do you love, and which do you hate?"

The woman said, "The younger of these two boys is my child

and the older is my husband's by his first wife. As their father lay dying he said to me, his wife, 'This child of mine has no mother, and I too am about to die. He will be all alone and have no one to look after him. Now that I am on the brink of death my mind dwells on him and I am troubled.' I replied, 'You may be sure that I will be as a mother to your child, just as you ask me to. You don't need to worry on his account.' The father heard these words and died happy. I cannot be false to them, and so I would rather that my own child be killed and my husband's child be allowed to go free."

Hearing her, the King was so moved by her faithfulness that he pardoned both, and the woman in great joy led the two sons back home.

The woman who would let her own son be killed to obtain the release of her stepson rather than break a promise had a rare heart. Everyone who heard of this praised her. So the tale's been told, and so it's been handed down.

Note to Story 4

1. Literally, "one was the mother's child and one was the father's child. When the father's child was young, both his father and mother died." What is meant here is children of the same father by different mothers.

44. HOW MO YEH OF CHINA MADE A SWORD AND PRESENTED IT TO THE KING AND HOW HIS SON, BROAD-OF-BROW, WAS KILLED

AT A TIME NOW PAST, in China [in which era is no longer known],[1] there was a man named Mo Yeh who was a smith. The King's consort could not bear the summer heat and constantly embraced an iron column. She became pregnant; when she gave birth, lo and behold! it was to an iron ball. The King was suspicious. "What's this!" he demanded. "I have done no wrong," replied the Queen; "It is only that I could not bear the summer heat and constantly embraced an iron column. Might that, I wonder, be the cause?" That was indeed the cause, the King decided.

He summoned the smith Mo Yeh and ordered him to make the iron ball into a precious sword.

Mo Yeh made two swords from the iron with which he was entrusted. He presented one to the King and hid the other. The King put the sword which Mo Yeh had given him among his treasures, but it continually cried out. Astounded, he asked his minister, "What is the meaning of the sword's crying?" The minister said, "The sword would not cry without a reason. The sword must surely have a mate; they are husband and wife, and it cries for love." Hearing this, the King fell into a rage. He instantly sent for Mo Yeh to punish him; but before his messenger could arrive Mo Yeh said to his wife, "Last night I saw an evil omen. I am certain that a messenger will come from the King and that I shall die. If the child with whom you are pregnant should be a boy, tell him, when he is grown, 'Look among the pines in the southern mountains.' " He left by the northern gate and went into the southern mountains. He hid in a great tree; and in the end he died.

Afterwards, his wife gave birth to a boy. When this child had reached his fifteenth year his forehead was so broad that his eyebrows were nine inches apart: he was therefore called Broad-of-Brow.[2] His mother recounted to him his father's parting injunctions in every particular. He went and looked as she had instructed him and found the sword. He took it, determined to wreak vengeance against his father's enemies.

Meanwhile, the King dreamed that there was a man whose eyebrows were nine inches apart and that this man was plotting against him and was going to kill him. He awoke in terror and sent a proclamation into every quarter of the kingdom: "Somewhere in the land there is a man whose eyebrows are nine inches apart. Whoever arrests him and succeeds in bringing me his head I will reward with a thousand pieces of gold."

In the natural course, Broad-of-Brow got wind of the proclamation and fled deep into the mountains. The minions who received the proclamation bestirred hands and feet and searched everywhere for him. In the mountains Broad-of-Brow encountered someone in the King's employ. The official saw that here was a man whose eyebrows were nine inches apart. Rejoicing, he inquired, "Are you the man named Broad-of-Brow?" "I am he," was the reply. The official said, "I and my fellows have been commanded to get your head and the sword you carry." Then and there Broad-of-Brow took the sword and cut off his own head and gave it to the official. The official carried it back to the palace and presented it to the King. The King gratefully rewarded him.

The King gave Broad-of-Brow's head to the official. "Destroy it at once by boiling," he commanded. Obedient, the official put the head in a kettle and boiled it for seven days; but after seven days it was still whole. He reported this to the King, who thought it strange and personally went to look in the pot. As the King peered inside his head dropped off, just like that. The two heads bit each other and fought with boundless ferocity. The official was flabbergasted. In the hope of weakening Broad-of-Brow's head he threw the sword into the pot. When he did so both heads disintegrated. The official also peered inside the pot, and his head also dropped off, just like that, and fell into the pot. The three heads all got mixed up together and no one could tell which was which. Therefore a single grave was made and the three heads were buried in it.

That grave exists even today, in a district called I-ch'un. So the tale's been told, and so it's been handed down.[3]

Notes to Story 44

1. Lacuna in the original; literally "in the —— era."

2. With some hesitation, as the compiler seems in search rather of a round number than of exact measurement, I have rendered *shaku* "nine inches," its presumed modern equivalent. The boy's name I have rendered freely; literally it is "Brows-a-*shaku*-apart."

3. As this story is a bit peculiar, it might be pointed out that avenging a father is a filial duty, hence its place among other stories illustrating filial conduct. Versions of this tale were very popular in Japan, appearing, for example, in the *Taiheiki* and *Soga monogatari*. Chinese predecessors can be found as early as the *Sou-shen chi* (ca. A.D. 300), a collection of tales of ghosts and the supernatural, but elements of the story must be even older. Chapter 6 of *Chuang Tzu* contains a reference to the famous sword [*sic*] Mo Yeh.

45. HOW HOU KU TRICKED HIS FATHER
AND PREVENTED AN UNFILIAL ACT

AT A TIME NOW PAST, in China [during which era is no longer known], there was a man of Ch'u whose name was Hou Ku. His father was unfilial and was angry with his own father for being slow to die.

Now, Hou Ku's father fashioned a litter and put his aged father in it. Hou Ku's father and Hou Ku carried it on their shoulders deep into the mountains, abandoned the old man, and returned home. Hou Ku brought the litter back with him. His father saw it and said, "What did you bring the litter back for?" Hou Ku answered, "I have just learned that a son is one who puts his aged father in a litter and abandons him in the mountains. That means that when my own father is old I will put him in a litter and abandon him in the mountains. This will save me from having to make a new one."

When his father heard this he thought, "I myself will be abandoned when I am old," and wild with anxiety he hurried back to the mountains to welcome his father back home. Thereafter, Hou Ku's father never stinted his filial care. This was due entirely to Hou Ku's scheme.

The whole world praises and admires Hou Ku beyond meaure: one who saves his grandfather's life and causes his own father to be a filial son truly deserves to be called wise. So the tale's been told, and so it's been handed down.[1]

Note to Story 45

1. The theme of this story is very popular, and versions of it can be found in the Indian and Japanese sections of *Konjaku* as well: Chapter Five, Story 22 (translated by Jones) and Chapter Thirty, Story 9 (translated by Brower).

Chapter Ten

1. HOW SHIH-HUANG OF CH'IN GOVERNED FROM HIS PALACE AT HSIEN-YANG

AT A TIME NOW PAST, in China, during the Ch'in dynasty, there lived a king named Shih-huang. He ruled fiercely and astutely, so that there was no one in all the land who did not obey him. Whoever displeased him in the slightest lost his head or had his hands or feet chopped off. And so, all men bent to his will as grasses before the wind.

To begin with, he constructed a palace at Hsien-yang and made it the place from which he governed. To the east of this palace was Han-ku Pass,[1] so called because it formed an enclosure like a box. To the north of his capital he constructed a high mountain. He built it to divide China from the land of the Hu barbarians and block any road by which the people of the Hu country could come into China. On the Chinese side it was like an ordinary mountain. People would go up it to amuse themselves. If they climbed to the very top — and what a ways that was — and looked toward the Hu country they could see everything that was there. On the side of the Hu country the mountain was perpendicular and plastered like a wall, so no one could go up it. From north to south the mountain was a thousand *li* long.[2] It was as high as the clouds. It was so high that the wild geese could not fly across it at the season when they migrate, so a hole was opened up inside it and then they flew through. That was because even in the open sky geese always fly in single file.

He . . . fear of the Hu country . . . decreed: "My sons and grandsons shall succeed one another as rulers of this country . . . must not know."[3] He said, "I will also get rid of everything that existed in bygone ages and make the laws anew. And I will also collect all the books from bygone ages and destroy them in the fire and make anew all the books that will be preserved for the future." And so some disciples of Confucius spirited away the noblest of the ancient books and hid them in a wall and plastered it over; thus they preserved them.

Now, Shih-huang had a horse on which he lavished affection day and night; its name was Tso-ts'an[4] and it was as strong as a dragon. Morning and evening he tended it lovingly. He dreamed that he had led it to the sea and was bathing it when a gigantic fish[5] suddenly came up out of the water, got Tso-ts'an in its mouth, and dragged the horse into the sea. Shih-huang awoke in utter terror. "What! Is the horse I cherish as my treasure to be eaten by a gigantic fish!" Enraged, he issued a proclamation throughout the land: "In the ocean there is a gigantic fish. Whoever shoots it and kills it will receive the reward he asks for." The people of the country heard the proclamation and went severally to the sea. They took ship and rowed far into the ocean, straining to see the fish; but though some caught faint glimpses of a gigantic fish, no one succeeded in shooting it. They returned to the King and told him, "When we gaze out into the ocean we see the fish, but even so we cannot shoot it. We are prevented by the dragon king."

Having heard this, the King wanted above all to be freed of his fear. He spoke to a master of the magic arts: "Go at once to the mountain of P'eng-lai[6] and fetch the medicine of immortality. True, no one has ever seen P'eng-lai, but even so, accounts of it have circulated from ancient times to the present day. Go quickly." The magician received this charge and immediately departed for P'eng-lai. A wait ensued. After many months he returned and told the King, "To get to P'eng-lai is in itself not easy. What's more, in the ocean there is a gigantic fish. I cannot reach the shores of P'eng-lai for fear of it." Hearing this, Shih-huang said, "That fish has come into these regions to injure me. It is all the more necessary for it to be killed." But though he issued proclamations, none of the people who went could shoot it.

Thereupon Shih-huang said, "I must hasten to the sea and shoot the fish myself." At once he . . . proceeding to that place . . . boarded a boat and [rowed] far out into the open sea until he saw [the fish].[7] Shih-huang rejoiced; he shot at the fish, his arrow struck it, and it died. As Shih-huang was returning in the midst of celebrations, he contracted a severe illness at a place called —— . Was it not because he had incurred censure from heaven? He called his son, the future Second Emperor, and his minister Chao Kao to his bedside and spoke to them in secret: "I have suddenly contracted a severe illness and I know that I must die. After my death, not one of my ministers or my hundred officials will accompany me back to my capital; they will all abandon me here and go away. And so, even though I am dead, do not let word of it get out here. Let me return to the capital inside my carriage just as though I were alive, and bury me there. I fear the humiliation of having my ministers and officials desert me on a journey. Do not disobey me in this." No sooner had he finished speaking than he died. In accordance with these last injunctions, the two men behaved on the return journey as though he were still living. At times when they would have reported to him they would pretend that he had spoken; and the two would confer and issue edicts.

It was summer, and as the days passed the stench within the carriage mounted. The two men consulted together and evolved a scheme: they immediately collected a great quantity of fish, of the kind called *hōgyo*.[8] They piled it on wagons fore and aft, attaching them to the front and back of the carriage in which Shih-huang was riding. The reason was that when this fish rotted its odor was unlike that of any other fish. The smell of decay within the carriage mingled with the smell of the fish, so that no one realized its cause. As Shih-huang had always been capricious when he was alive, nobody thought it at all peculiar. After some days they reached the capital and prepared a grave; it was only then that the people learned of his death.

After that his son ascended the throne as Second Emperor. He consulted with his minister Chao Kao on all matters of government; but he thought, "My father Shih-huang ruled exactly as he pleased and followed his own judgment in everything. Why shouldn't I do as he did?" As he governed, differences arose between him and Chao Kao. Chao Kao thought, "This king is Shih-huang's son; for all that, he has only been on the throne a short time. If the bond between us is already so slight, how much the worse will it be for me when he has been on the throne longer!" With this, he conceived the idea of insurrection. But he did not know the temper of the people, and he was extremely doubtful, so he thought he would test their sympathies.

He led a stag out in front of the King and said, "What a horse this is!" The King looked at it and said, "This is a stag, not a horse." Chao Kao said, "It's a horse; what else could it be? Ask the people." The King questioned his subjects, and everyone who saw the animal said, "It's not a stag, it's a horse." "Aha!" thought

Chao Kao, "the people are all on my side. I can revolt without fear." He secretly raised and equipped a large army, and spying out the other's weaknesses and weighing opportunities, he entered the royal palace and abused the King.

Hearing his accusations, the King thought, "Even though I am king I have not ruled long; my throne is not secure and the force at my command is slight. Chao Kao is my subject, but for years he has bent the world to his will, and his might is awesome. Well then, I shall flee." He stole out of the capital and secluded himself in a place called Wang-i Palace. Chao Kao went there with a large army, surrounded the palace, and laid siege. The King's army resisted, but as its strength was inferior, it could not defend him. The minister's army attacked strongly. The King was at his wits' end; he said, "O my minister, spare my life. From now on, I will neglect nothing that might please you. I won't be king any more; just let me serve you as your minister." Chao Kao would not give in and pressed him harshly. Then the King said, "In that case, make me the ruler of a small province and send me far away. But let me live." Chao Kao upbraided him without relenting. The King said, "Then let me become an ordinary man, without office of any kind. Cast me out. Make me a nobody. Just let me live!" He pleaded desperately, but the minister would give no quarter; inexorable, the minister struck him down. Thereupon Chao Kao led his army back to the capital.

After that, Chao Kao set Shih-huang's grandson Tzu Ying on the throne. Tzu Ying thought to himself, "I'm thankful that I've ascended the throne and will rule the land, but my uncle the Second Emperor, for all that he was king, was killed by Chao Kao. He did not reign long. Am I not like him? If I differ in the slightest with Chao Kao he will kill me; of that I cannot doubt." With this realization, he secretly got up a plot and killed Chao Kao.

Though he now ruled without fear, Tzu Ying was all alone. A man named Hsiang Yü saw how few his supporters were and came and killed him. The palace at Hsien-yang was destroyed, and Shih-huang's. . . . The royal residence of Ch'in went up in flames. The fire burned for three months. Tzu Ying had been on the throne for forty-six days. With that the Ch'in dynasty was destroyed. So the tale's been told, and so it's been handed down.

Notes to Story 1

Chapter Ten 75

Notes to Story 1

1. The incidents that form this story all have their source in the sixth chapter of the *Shih chi* ("Records of the Historian") of Ssu-ma Ch'ien (translated in Édouard Chavannes, *Les mémoires historiques de Se-ma Ts'ien* (Paris: E. Leroux, 1895–1905), vol. 5); but either the *Konjaku* compiler's memory was faulty or he learned the story from some oral retelling. One of the interesting aspects of this account of the First Emperor of China is the opportunity it gives to see history being turned into legend, for *Konjaku's* description of the Great Wall is even more marvelous than the original. The explanation of the name Han-ku Pass must have mystified early readers of *Konjaku,* but here the cause is not imagination but scribal error. Han-ku is indeed ordinarily written with characters that mean "box and "valley"; here, however, another character, which in Japan would have the same pronunciation as the first of these but has an entirely different meaning, has been substituted for it.

2. The *li* of Ch'in times has been estimated at 405 meters.

3. Ellipsis points indicate damage to the text.

4. Tso-ts'an means the horse at the left of a team; the *Konjaku* compiler, however, seems to be using the expression as a proper noun.

5. The expression, literally "a fish called 'tall, great fish' " is peculiar and perhaps should be taken, if not as a proper noun, as the name of a species (though imaginary and with only one member). "Tall" (*kō* in Japanese, Chinese *kao*) may have been a substitution by the Japanese scribe or compiler for Chinese *chiao,* with which, in Japanese pronunciation, it would have been homophonous. The modern meaning of *chiao* is shark; its meaning in ancient times, however, is not certain. The entire passage is compounded of two incidents that are separate in the *Shih chi:* in one, Ch'in Shih Huang-ti shoots a *chiao* fish, with dire results; in the other, his son, the Second Emperor, dreams that his horse Tso-ts'an is dragged into the sea by a white tiger.

6. One of the three magic mountains, abodes of Taoist immortals, thought to rise as islands in the eastern sea.

7. Brackets in this sentence indicate reconstruction of the damaged text, where it has been possible.

8. Again there is a question of meaning, arising from the substitution of a character. The compound here seems to be the name of a species which might be interpreted literally as "square-fish" or, more likely, "regional-fish." But *hō-* (Chinese *fang*) was very likely used as a homophone, in Japanese pronunciation, for Chinese *pao,* the character in the *Shih chi.* What kind of fish covered the decaying corpse of the First Emperor? The character read *pao* can denote abalone, catfish, or a variety of salmon. A conventional interpretation, which the modern Jap-

anese commentator suggests is applicable here also, is that it can simply
mean rotting fish. But the text that follows, which says that this fish
smelled worse than other kinds when it rotted, implies that the *Konjaku* compiler thought of it as some specific variety.

8. HOW WU CHAO-HSIAO OF CHINA
SAW A POEM ON THE WATER
AND LOVED ITS AUTHOR

AT A TIME NOW PAST, in China [during which reign is no longer
known], there lived a man of great understanding named Wu
Chao-hsiao.

In his youth he once was strolling along the banks of a stream
that issued from within the walls of the imperial palace, when he
saw a leaf floating downwards on the current. He picked it up and
examined it: it was a persimmon leaf, reddened by the frost, and it
bore a poem. The poem, he saw, was in a woman's handwriting.
"Who could have written it?" he wondered. He did not know
who she was, but imagining her temperament and everything
about her, he fell hopelessly in love. In the end, for lack of any
way of meeting her, he composed a poem to the same rhymes,
wrote it too on a persimmon leaf, went to the head of the stream,
and floated it on the water so that the current would bear it inside
the palace walls. As often as he was oppressed by his love for her,
Chao-hsiao would take out the persimmon leaf poem he had
found and read it, and his tears would flow.

Thus the years passed. Sequestered within the palace walls
were numerous ladies who had spent long years in vain, for the
Emperor had never once deigned to look upon them. The Emperor said, "These women have wasted their lives in my household, and I feel very sorry for them. Let some few be sent back to
their parents and be found ordinary husbands." So he commanded, whereupon a few were sent home.

Now, among the concubines whom the Emperor graciously
returned was one who was exceptionally beautiful. Her parents
were still living and they married her to Chao-hsiao. He, for his
part, loved only the woman who had written the poem, even
though she was unknown to him. He had had no thought of ever

approaching another; nevertheless, since it was the parents' doing, he unwillingly became a bridegroom. His wife seemed to care for him, and it pained him that he could not love her. Once, briefly, he forgot about the author of the persimmon leaf poem for whom he had yearned day and night, and his wife said to him, "You have had a strangely preoccupied air. Is something wrong? Tell me; keep nothing back." Chao-hsiao replied, "Long ago, as I was strolling by the stream outside the palace walls, I saw a leaf floating upon the water. I picked it up and examined it. It was a persimmon leaf, reddend by the frost. There was a poem on it in a woman's handwriting. I longed to see the writer, but since I did not know who she was, I had no way of finding her or any means of meeting her. Even today I have not forgotten her. But now that you and I have become intimate, my longing has unexpectedly been soothed."

Hearing this, the woman said, "How did that poem go? More-over, did you not compose one to the same rhymes?" "It went like this," Chao-hsiao replied. "I let my imagination dwell on the woman within the palace who composed it. I went to the head of the stream, composed a poem to the same rhymes, and set it afloat in the hope that it might somehow come her way." Hearing this, the woman shed tears, for she knew now how deep was the bond between them. "It was I who wrote that poem," she told Chao-hsiao, "and later I discovered the answering poem. I have it by me even now." Each took out the poem that he cherished, and each saw that it was in the other's hand. And so they knew that their intimacy was not of this life only and, amidst tears, vowed their love for each other all the more tenderly.

The woman said, "This is how I came to write the poem. I had entered the palace in obedience to a royal command, but I had never once appeared before the Emperor. In sorrow over the months and days I had passed in fruitless waiting, I went for a stroll along the banks of a stream. I composed a poem, wrote it on a persimmon leaf, and floated it upon the water. Later, as I was again walking along the banks, I saw a leaf lodged by the current among the rocks and picked it up. It was a persimmon leaf, and someone had written a poem on it. I thought that the author must have been the person who had found the poem that I had written, and I saved it." The husband's feelings when he heard this must have been more than he could bear.

And thus, both realized that the bond between husband and wife comes from our karma from past lives. So the tale's been told, and so it's been handed down.

12. HOW CHUANG TZU WENT TO SOMEONE'S HOUSE, AND HOW HIS HOST KILLED A GOOSE TO SERVE WITH THE WINE

AT A TIME NOW PAST, in China, there was a man named Chuang Tzu. His mind was sagacious and his understanding broad.

Once, as he was going along the road, he passed through a stand of timber. Among the many trees was one, all gnarled and twisted, that had attained a great age. Chuang Tzu asked the woodsman, "How is it that this tree has stayed alive to such a great age?" The woodsman replied, "I choose trees for cutting that are well formed and straight. This tree is gnarled and twisted. Since it is no good for anything, I have not cut it, and thus it has attained its great age." "How very true," thought Chuang Tzu, and went on his way.

The next day Chuang Tzu went to someone's house. The master of the house set out a fine meal for him. First he served wine, but there were no tidbits to accompany it. The household had two geese, and the host ordered, "Kill one of the geese and make some tidbits." The servant charged with tending the geese said, "Which should I kill? The one that sings nicely, or the one that doesn't sing?" The host said, "Let the singing one live to sing; kill the one that doesn't sing and make it into tidbits." The servant did as his master instructed, twisted the neck of the goose that didn't sing, and prepared tidbits.

Thereupon Chuang Tzu said, "The tree in the stand of timber I saw yesterday had been let live because it was useless. Today my host has spared the life of a goose because it has a talent. This proves that whether you live or die does not depend on whether you are wise or foolish: it is something that just comes about of itself. Nor can we deduce a rule that those who have talent will not die or that those who are useless will not die. The useless tree lives long; the goose that did not sing died at once. Such is life."

This was a saying of Chuang Tzu. So the tale's been told, and so it's been handed down.

13. HOW CHUANG TZU OBSERVED THE BEHAVIOR OF DUMB CREATURES AND FLED

AT A TIME NOW PAST, in China, there was a man named Chuang Tzu. His mind was sagacious and his understanding broad.

Once, as he was going along the road, he saw a heron standing in the marsh with its eye on something. Chuang Tzu thought he would sneak up on the heron and kill it with a blow. He went up to it, stick in hand, but the heron did not try to escape. Chuang Tzu was astonished; coming ever closer, he saw that the heron was standing there to catch a prawn. He knew that it did not know that a man was going to deal it a blow. And when he looked at the prawn that the heron was trying to catch he saw that it, too, did not try to escape. It was trying to catch a tiny bug and did not know that the heron was watching it.

Then and there, Chuang Tzu threw away his stick and fled, for he thought to himself, "Neither the heron nor the prawn knows that someone is going to harm it. Each thinks only of harming another. I likewise was going to kill the heron. For all I know there might be a being superior to me who is going to harm me. I'll run away to prevent that," and he took to his heels. That was very wise. Everyone should think as he did.

On another occasion, as Chuang Tzu and his wife were looking out upon the water together, they saw a large fish sporting near the surface. His wife said, "That fish must surely be enjoying itself; it plays so exuberantly." Chuang Tzu responded, "How do you know how a fish thinks?" His wife replied, "How do you know whether I know how a fish thinks?" Whereupon Chuang Tzu said, "Since you are not a fish, you do not know how a fish thinks. Since you are not I, you do not know how I think." That was very wise. Truly no one knows another's heart or mind, no matter how intimate they may be.

Both Chuang Tzu and his wife were sagacious and had profound understanding. So the tale's been told, and so it's been handed down.[1]

Note to Story 13

1. This story and the one preceding are both based, directly and indirectly, on anecdotes in the *Chuang Tzu*. Amusingly, in the *Chuang Tzu* text of the final episode recounted here, the speakers are not Chuang Tzu and his wife but Chuang Tzu and Hui Tzu; and the arguments given to Chuang Tzu there are those given to his wife in *Konjaku*, while those of Hui Tzu are given by *Konjaku* to Chuang Tzu. But Chuang Tzu wins the argument anyway, insisting that Hui Tzu knew that Chuang Tzu was right before beginning to question him. See Burton Watson, tr., *The Complete Works of Chuang Tzu* (New York: Columbia University Press, 1968), pp. 188–189.

Tales of Buddhism in Japan

In Chapter Eleven, devoted to the founding of Buddhism in Japan, appear accounts of such famous early patriarchs of that religion as the magician E no Ubasoku and the pilgrim Dōshō. The miracle tales in Chapters Twelve through Seventeen are of varied types. Some, like the story of Shunchō, are simple glorifications of the sutras, and the persons in them are not so much stereotypes as abstractions. Others are stories of escape, whether from supernatural harm or down-to-earth dangers; here, as in the best of the tales of those who become victims in this present life but are helped to a better rebirth in the afterlife, it is the human dimensions of the experience that are the focus of the storytelling. The tale of the monk who takes refuge under the great bell of a temple called Dōjōji is one of the most famous of all Japanese legends; in later times this legend provided the theme for both *nō* and *kabuki* dramas. The apparent sinner who is a saint in secret is a stock figure of Japanese hagiography, but such a one has rarely been depicted more skillfully or with more genuine sympathy than in the story of the priest who ate carrion; while most readers will find the picture of monastic life offered by the story of the monk who begot gold rather a wry one. Chapter Eighteen is lacking. The first half of Chapter Nineteen consists of stories of religious conversions; in the example translated here, conversion appears in combination with another common Buddhist theme, the injunction against wanton killing of living creatures. Most of the remainder of this chapter, and Chapter Twenty, give instruction in the principle that good and bad deeds are rewarded and punished by karma; especially in the story of Shinkai, the compiler clearly relished his task of portraying the outrageous behavior that led to condign punishment.

Chapter Eleven

3. HOW E NO UBASOKU RECITED SPELLS AND EMPLOYED DEMONIC DEITIES

AT A TIME NOW PAST, in our own country, in the reign of Emperor [Monmu],[1] there was a holy man named E no Ubasoku.[2] He came from the village of Chihara in Upper Kazuraki District in Yamato Province, and his clan name in secular life was Kamo E. For more than forty years he lived on Mount Kazuraki, wisteria bark his clothing, pine needles his food, and a mountain cave his home. He bathed in pure springs, cleansed his heart of defilement, and recited the spell of the Peacock King.[3] There were times when, riding upon a cloud of five colors, he visited the grottoes of the immortals. By night he summoned to his service demonic deities and made them draw water and gather firewood. All beings obeyed him.

Now, the Bodhisattva Zaō of Mount Mitake[4] appeared in response to Ubasoku's devotions. Ubasoku therefore journeyed back and forth continually between Mount Kazuraki and Mount Mitake. In consequence, he assembled the demonic deities and said to them: ["Build a bridge from Mount Kazuraki to Mount Mitake for me to travel on"]. When they heard this, the demonic deities [all raised their voices][5] in lamentation, but he would not give way. They were vexed beyond measure, but they could not escape his torments, and so they brought together a great many boulders and began to erect a bridge. The demonic deities told Ubasoku, however: "We are hideous to look upon. We shall therefore build this bridge under concealment of night." Night after night they made haste to build. Ubasoku, however, summoned Hitokotonushi, the god of Kazuraki. "Why should you be ashamed to show yourself?" he said. "If that's how you feel about it, we won't build the bridge at all!" replied the god. Enraged, E no Ubasoku trussed the god up with spells and confined him in the bottom of a valley.

Subsequently Hitokotonushi entered into someone in the capital and speaking through this medium lodged an accusation: "E no Ubasoku has treacherous designs and is plotting to overturn the state." When the Emperor heard about this he was alarmed and despatched an official to arrest Ubasoku, but Ubasoku flew up into the sky and could not be caught. The official thereupon arrested Ubasoku's mother. At the sight of his mother taken prisoner, he came forth of his own accord to be made prisoner in her stead. The Emperor pondered his offense and exiled him to the island of Ōshima off the coast of Izu Province. An island it might be; but he ran about on the surface of the ocean as though on dry land, and among the mountain peaks he flew just like a bird. During daylight he observed his exile out of respect for the throne, but by night he traveled to Mount Fuji in Suruga Province. He prayed that he might be released from his punishment. After three years, the Emperor heard that he was guiltless and summoned him to the capital. . . .

[The story breaks off here. We know from other tales that E no Ubasoku then went to the Chinese continent.]

Notes to Story 3

1. Reigned 697–707; lacuna in the original.

2. He is also known as E no Gyōja, E no Shōkaku, and E no Ozunu. Ubasoku is the Japanese form of Sanskrit *upāsaka,* a lay devotee. His clan name, E, is also often read En; hence En no Ubasoku, etc.

3. The Peacock King is one of the Four Guardian Kings, supernatural protectors of the Dharma who are worshipped in the Tantric schools of Buddhism. The magical formulae associated with him were considered especially efficacious in averting natural calamity.

4. Zaō is a deity of hybrid Indo-Japanese origin; the mountain of which he is the patron is the highest peak in the Yoshino range and one of the holy mountains of the Shugendō cult, which considers E no Ubasoku its patriarch.

5. The general sense of these two lacunae can be reconstructed from other versions of the story.

4. HOW THE VENERABLE DŌSHŌ WENT TO CHINA, WAS TRANSMITTED THE HOSSŌ TEACHINGS, AND RETURNED HOME

AT A TIME NOW PAST, in our own country, in the reign of Emperor Tenji, there was a holy man named the Venerable Dōshō. His clan name in secular life was Funa,[1] and he came from Kōchi Province. In youth he renounced secular life and became a monk of the Gankōji. His understanding was broad and his mind upright; he was rich in piety and as worthy as a very Buddha. Therefore, everyone from the Emperor on down, persons of high and low degree, monks and laymen alike, women as well as men, bowed low before him and revered him beyond measure.

Now the Emperor summoned Dōshō and said to him, "Recently I have heard reports that in China there is a holy monk named Hsüan-tsang Tripitaka.[2] He has gone to India and brought back orthodox teachings. Among the teachings that were transmitted to him is that of the Mahāyāna school called 'Consciousness Only;'[3] to study it has been his special delight. 'The elements of phenomenal existence are inseparable from consciousness' is the tenet by which this school teaches the way to enlightenment. This teaching, however, does not yet exist in our country. Go straightway to China, meet Hsüan-tsang, and learn the doctrine from him so that you may bring it back."

Having received the imperial decree, Dōshō crossed the sea to China. Upon arriving at Hsüan-tsang's monastery he stationed himself at the gate and sent someone in to announce him. "I am a monk who has come from Japan at the command of my country's king." The messenger returned and asked his reasons for coming. "My king has commanded me to acquire the teachings of the school of Consciousness Only," Dōshō replied.

When Hsüan-tsang heard the report, he immediately called Dōshō in and came down from his seat to welcome him personally into his chamber. The two chatted face to face as though they were old acquaintances. Thereafter Hsüan-tsang instructed Dōshō in Consciousness Only. Dōshō would return to his cell each night; during the day he would visit Hsüan-tsang. This went on for a year, until all the doctrines of the school had been transmitted to him as thoroughly as when water is poured from one jug into another. When he was about to return home, Hsüan-tsang's disciples said to their master, "You have a goodly number of disciples in this country, and all are men of outstanding merit. Yet you honor none of them; but when you saw this monk who had come from Japan you came down from your seat and did him reverence. We do not understand. Even supposing that he is worthy, he comes from a small country. What can he amount to, after all? He'll never be a match for a Chinese." Hsüan-tsang replied, "Go to the Japanese monk's chamber this very night and secretly observe him. You will see whether he is to be disparaged or praised."

Two or three of Hsüan-tsang's disciples went to Dōshō's cell at night and spied on him as he sat reading the sutras. They watched him closely and saw him emit a white light some five or six feet long from his mouth. They were amazed. . . . "This is a marvel. Our master [was quite right to favor him],"[4] they decided. "Moreover, the fact that our master knew in advance the meritoriousness of a stranger from another land shows that he himself is a manifestation of the Buddha." They returned to their master and said, "As we secretly watched, the Japanese monk emitted a light from his mouth." "What fools you are!" said Hsüan-tsang. "You spoke ill of him without thinking that I might have good reason to honor him." The disciples withdrew in shame.

Something else told of Dōshō's Chinese sojourn is that he journeyed to the country of Silla at the invitation of five hundred eminent monks. As he was preaching in a monastery on the Lotus Sutra he heard someone in the room ask a question in the language of our own country. In the pulpit Dōshō paused in his explication of the Dharma to ask "Who are you?" A voice replied, "I am E no Ubasoku, formerly of Japan. The gods of Japan have all gone mad, and the people have evil minds, so I came away. Even now, however, I visit there from time to time." Upon hearing that this was someone who was once of our own country, Dōshō decided that he must see him face to face. He stepped down from the pulpit to look for him, but no one could be found. Dōshō returned to China in bitter disappointment.[5]

After Dōshō had completed his studies and returned to Japan, he instructed his numerous disciples in the principles of Consciousness Only, and this teaching which he transmitted to them has been handed down uninterruptedly and flourishes even today. Moreover, he built a Meditation Cloister, as it is called and

dwelled there. As his life neared its end he bathed, put on pure
clothing, and faced the west, sitting upright in the posture for
meditation. As he was doing so a great light filled the room.
Dōshō opened his eyes. "Do you see a light?" he asked his disciples. "We do," they replied. "Don't let word of it get out," Dōshō
said. Afterwards, in the night, the light went forth from his
chamber and shone upon the trees in the temple courtyard.
There it lingered, and then it flew away toward the west. The
awe and dread of the disciples as they beheld it exceeded all
bounds. Dōshō had died while seated facing the west, in the
posture for meditation. From these signs they knew for certain
that he had gone to paradise. His Meditation Cloister is in the
southeast part of the Gankōji.

The Venerable Dōshō was indeed a manifestation of the Buddha. So the tale's been told, and so it's been handed down.

Notes to Story 4

1. Tenji (the more usual reading is Tenchi), r. 668–671. Dōshō, 629–700,
was famous for a number of reasons: he introduced the practice of
cremation to Japan, and since he built a meditation cloister, later ages
credited him with having been the first to bring Zen to Japan. In actuality Dōshō's journey to China took place in 653. Some commentators
read his secular clan name as Tan.

2. Hsüan-tsang (nicknamed Tripitaka because of his work as a translator
of scripture) was a pilgrim to India from 629 to 645; his adventures
inspired the novel *Hsi-yü chi*. There is an account of his life by Arthur
Waley, in *The Real Tripitaka and Other Pieces* (London: George Allen
and Unwin, 1952), pp. 9–130. The Japanese saw in Dōshō's pilgrimage
to China to study with Hsüan-tsang a parallel to Hsüan-tsang's own
heroic journey.

3. An idealistic Mahayana school based on the texts that Hsüan-tsang
brought back and translated; the Hossō (Chinese, Fa-hsiang) of the title
is another name for it.

4. There are two lacunae here; words in brackets are a guess at recon-
structing the second one, based on other versions of the story.

5. The legend of this meeting was well known but contradicts chronol-
ogy (see 11:3, note 1), as historians have pointed out since at least the
fourteenth century.

Chapter Twelve

28. HOW A GOVERNMENT CLERK OF HIGO PROVINCE ESCAPED A RAKSHASA

AT A TIME NOW PAST, in Higo Province, there was a government clerk. He went each day to the government office where he performed his duties; he had been doing this for some years. On one occasion an urgent matter arose and he set out from his home early in the morning. He was on horseback and without a single attendant. The office was scarcely a mile from his home, so that as a rule he arrived there after a short time, but today the farther he went the farther away it became. Unable to get there, he lost his way entirely and came out upon a broad plain. Where he was, he did not know. He had ridden all day, and now the sun had set. There was nowhere to spend the night; all was open plain.

In his distress he kept hoping to come upon some human habitation; and then, from an outcropping of the foothills, he caught a faint glimpse of the corner of a prosperous-looking dwelling. "I must have come near a settlement," he thought, and hurried joyfully toward it. When he examined the house from close by, however, there was no sign of human beings. He went all around it. "Is anyone there? Come out, please. What is the name of this place?" From within a woman answered, "Who are you, sir? Come right in, sir!" At the sound of her voice the clerk was terrified, but he said, "I've lost my way. I've urgent business, so I can't come in. Just tell me how to find the road." "Wait a moment," said the woman, "I'll come out and show you." His fear mounted, and he wheeled his horse about and began to flee. Hearing the hoofbeats, the woman cried "Wait, wait!" Looking back, he saw her come out; she stood as high as the eaves of the house and her eyes glowed light. "So it was, indeed! I came to the house of an oni,"[1] he thought, and applied the whip. "Why are you trying to run away?" said the woman. "Stop this instant, you!" To say that he was terrified would scarcely suffice. His head swam; he felt as though his guts would split. He saw a being ten feet tall; fire issued from its eyes and mouth, brilliant as lightning; its mouth was wide open, and it was striking its hands together as it pursued him. His senses all but failed him at the sight, and he would have fallen from his horse; but he whipped it onward and onward again, praying: "Kannon save me! Save my life, even for just one day!" The horse stumbled and fell. The clerk was thrown free in front of it. Now surely the creature would catch him and devour him, he thought. There was a cave close by, and he ran in, beside himself with fear.

The oni came hot on his tracks. "Hey, where'd he go? He was here a moment ago," it said, but instead of going to look for him, it first ate his horse. The clerk heard everything, and he had not the slightest doubt that as soon as it had finished with the horse it would eat him. Was there a chance that it did not know he was in the cave? All he could do was pray. "Kannon save me!"

Now, when the oni was through eating the horse it came up to the mouth of the cave and said, "This man is supposed to be my supper today. Why won't you give him back? You're always doing things like that. It's not fair. You're mean to me." "I thought I'd found a place to hide, but it knows I'm here," thought the clerk. From within the cave came a voice: "He'll be my supper today. You can't have him. You've had the horse and that's enough." "There's no way I can survive now," thought the clerk. "The oni that chased me was dreadful enough, but there is one in this cave who is even more terrible. It is certain to eat me," and his distress was boundless. "Even though I pray to Kannon, my life will soon be over. This must be because of the sins of my previous lives."

The oni outside the cave earnestly repeated its pleas, but the one within would not yield, and the clerk heard the one outside return home, whining. Now, surely, the other would drag him off and devour him, he thought. But just then the voice in the cave said, "Today you would have been eaten by an oni, but by virtue of your fervent prayers to Kannon you have escaped harm. Hereafter you must devote yourself to the Buddha with all your heart and recite the Lotus Sutra. Now then, do you know who it is that speaks to you?" The clerk replied that he did not. The voice said, "I am no oni. Once, long ago, a holy man lived in this cave. On a peak to the west he built a reliquary mound, burying under it a copy of the Lotus Sutra. Year upon year has passed since then, and mound and sutra both have crumbled away. All that remains is the first character of the title, *Myō*. That first character is none other than I, myself. During my time here I have rescued nine hundred and ninety-nine persons who would have been eaten by the oni. You are the thousandth. Leave this place at once and go home. Strive always to worship the Buddha and recite the Lotus Sutra." The clerk was sent home, with a beautiful boy to escort him.[2]

Weeping and performing reverent salutations, the clerk followed the boy and regained his home. The boy saw him to the gate and said, "Have single-minded faith; recite the Lotus Sutra" — and then the boy vanished. The clerk wept and made obeisance; it was midnight when he returned home. He told his parents and his wife and children everything, and they were profoundly moved. Thereafter, arousing earnest faith, the clerk recited the Lotus Sutra and was all the more fervent in worshiping Kannon.

Now think: though only one character of the Lotus Sutra remained, it saved a man's life. You can imagine, then, the merit that will come from copying the Lotus Sutra in the prescribed form and with true faith. If such is the benefit in this present life, do not doubt that you will escape all torments in the life to come. So the tale's been told, and so it's been handed down.

Notes to Story 28

1. She is called a rakshasa in the title. Japanese dictionaries define a *rasetsu* (rakshasa) as an evil oni that eats people. All oni, however, are evil and eat people. In the story's presumed source, *Dai Nihon Hokke genki,* she appears in the text as a *rasetsu.* See Dykstra, "Miraculous Tales of the Lotus Sutra," pp. 204–205.

2. This refers to a special kind of supernatural being, the *gohō dōshi* or *gohō tendō,* the "divine boy who protects the Dharma." These beings are the messengers of the divinities who uphold the Buddha's teaching; they also make themselves servants of religious adepts, and in *setsuwa* they are often given the task of escorting home persons who have strayed into fairyland. A divine boy appears in the next story, also.

Chapter Thirteen

10. HOW THE SUTRA CHANTER SHUNCHŌ EXHIBITED THE LOTUS SUTRA'S EFFICACY

AT A TIME NOW PAST, there was a sutra chanter named Shun-chō. He chanted the Lotus Sutra day and night. He had no fixed home but drifted from place to place, doing nothing but read aloud the sutra. His heart was full of compassion: when he witnessed another's suffering, he felt it as his suffering, and when he witnessed another's joy he felt it as his own happiness.

Now Shunchō saw the jails in the east and west parts of the capital and sighed with pity. "These prisoners," he thought, "have brought punishment on themselves by their transgressions. Even so — if I could somehow contrive to plant in them the seeds of Buddhahood, I could free them of their pain. If they die in prison, in their next lives they will doubtless fall into the Three Evil Paths.[1] I will therefore commit a crime on purpose, so as to be caught and put in prison. There I shall zealously chant the Lotus Sutra that they may hear it." He went to the house of a certain nobleman and stole a single gold-and-silver vessel. He took it forthwith to a gambling house and staked it in a game of *suguroku,* so that everyone would see it. The people who were gathered there became suspicious. "That looks like the vessel that disappeared from his lordship So-and-So's house," they said. They raised such a clamor that the word spread, and Shunchō was arrested and questioned. His guilt was obvious, and he was put in jail. He went to jail gladly; and to fulfill his purpose he chanted the Lotus Sutra with all his heart. The prisoners who heard his voice were many, and all shed tears and bowed their heads in reverence. Shunchō rejoiced inwardly and chanted day and night.

Now, from the cloistered emperor and his ladies and the highest nobles there came letters to the Chief of the Imperial Police, saying: "Shunchō has for many years been a reciter of the Lotus Sutra. He must by no means be put to torture." Moreover, the Chief in a dream saw the Bodhisattva Fugen mounted on a white elephant, with a halo of light, bearing in his hands a bowl of rice.

Fugen was standing at the prison gate looking in, and when someone asked, "Why do you stand here?" replied, "Shunchō, the chanter of the Lotus Sutra, is in prison. I come each day to make a gift to him." Awakening, the Chief was overcome with dread, and he sent Shunchō forth from the prison. In this manner, Shunchō was jailed five or six times and released each time without interrogation.

Shunchō committed more crimes and once again was arrested. On this occasion, the Imperial Police met in their headquarters and decided: "Shunchō is a hardened criminal, yet he is always let off without interrogation, and so he goes on stealing to his heart's content. This time he must be punished with the utmost severity. His feet will be cut off, and he will be made a bondsman." The officers led him out to the palace guards' riding grounds at First Avenue. Just as they were preparing to cut off his feet, Shunchō raised his voice and chanted the Lotus Sutra. The officers wept to hear it and were filled with awe. They therefore let Shunchō go free. And again, their Chief had a dream in which he saw a boy flawlessly beautiful, in full court dress, his hair dressed in loops in childish fashion.[2] The boy came to him and said, "The holy man Shunchō commits crimes on purpose, in order to save the criminals in the prisons. He has been seven times a prisoner. He teaches by expedient means, as did the Buddha himself." Awakening, the Chief was overcome all the more with dread.

With no place to dwell, Shunchō finally died in a hut near the paddocks on First Avenue. His skull remained, for there was no one to dispose of it. Every night, people who lived nearby would hear a voice chanting the Lotus Sutra. They were filled with reverence, but they had no idea who it was, and they thought it very strange. Then a holy man came and took the skull to bury deep in the mountains. Thereafter the chanting ceased. And so they realized that it had been the skull that chanted.

The holy man Shunchō was no mere man but a manifestation of the Buddha. So people said at the time. So the tale's been told, and so it's been handed down.

Notes to Story 10

1. The three kinds of subhuman rebirth, minus that of asura.

2. A typical description of a divine boy.

39. ABOUT TWO MEN IN IZUMO PROVINCE, RECITERS OF THE WREATH AND LOTUS SUTRAS

AT A TIME NOW PAST, in Izumo Province, there were two holy men. One recited the Wreath Sutra and was called Hōgon, "Dharma Wreath." The other recited the Lotus Sutra, and his name was Renzō, "Lotus Storehouse." The pair had formerly been monks of the Daianji, but each, through some circumstance, had left his temple and had come to this province to live. Both were pure in body and upright in mind.

Now Hōgon had been reciting the Wreath Sutra for twenty years, but all the while he was obliged to worry continually about obtaining his daily food. A Dharma-protecting deity assumed human form, came to him, and said, "I shall be your patron and make you a daily offering. Trouble yourself about food no longer. Devote yourself single-mindedly to the sacred teachings." The holy man was overjoyed. Receiving his daily offering, he ceased his complaining. After some days he said to the deity, "Tomorrow morning please bring a meal for two. I should like to invite the Lotus Sutra chanter to eat with me." The deity assented. The next morning, Hōgon invited Renzō, and Renzō hurried to him. They waited for the food, but nothing at all appeared. The time that scripture appoints for eating passed, and at sundown Renzō returned home.

It was then that the deity brought the food. He said to Hōgon, "I tried to come this morning as you told me to yesterday; but when I arrived Brahma, Indra, the Four Deva Kings, and the Holy Throng of Bodhisattvas who guard the Lotus Sutra were crowding about the Lotus Sutra chanter from every quarter. I could scarcely get near—let alone make my way through! I've been waiting with my offering since morning. When the Lotus Sutra holy man went away, the deities went with him. I came the moment I could." Hearing this, Hōgon knew that he had witnessed a marvel and was filled with awe. He himself prepared an offering of food, took it to Renzō, and presented it with reverent salutations.

Thereafter Hōgon, realizing the supreme excellence of the Lotus Sutra, added it to his recitations and acknowledged himself Renzō's disciple. So the tale's been told, and so it's been handed down.

Chapter Fourteen

3. HOW A MONK OF THE DŌJŌJI IN THE PROVINCE OF KII COPIED THE LOTUS SUTRA AND BROUGHT SALVATION TO SERPENTS

AT A TIME NOW PAST, there were two monks on pilgrimage to Kumano. One was well along in years; the other was young and extraordinarily good-looking. When they came to Muro District, the two of them rented lodgings and settled down for the night. The owner of the house was a widow and young, with two or three maids her only companions. When this woman saw the handsome young monk who had taken lodgings with her, her lustful desires were deeply aroused. She tended assiduously to his comfort. Night fell, and the monks went to bed. At midnight she secretly crept to where the young monk was sleeping, covered him with her dress, and lay down beside him. She nudged him awake; he opened his eyes in fright and confusion. "I never give lodging to travelers," said the woman, "but I let you stay here tonight because from the time I first saw you, this afternoon, I have longed to make you my spouse. I thought that by taking you in for the night I would achieve my aim, and now I have come to you. My husband is dead and I am a widow. Take pity on me!" Hearing her, the monk got up, terrified. He replied, "I have a long-standing vow; in accordance with it, in recent days I have purified myself in mind and body and set out on the distant journey to present myself before the deity of Kumano.[1] Should I carelessly break my vow here, the consequences would be dreadful for both of us. Abandon all such thoughts at once." He refused with all the strength at his command. The woman was greatly vexed, and all night long she kept embracing him and teasing and fondling him. The monk tried this argument and that argument to soothe her. "It is not that I refuse, my lady. But just now I'm on a pilgrimage to Kumano. I'll spend a few days there offering lamps and paper strips. Then, when I've turned homeward, I will do as you ask," he promised. The woman believed him and went back to her own bed. At daybreak the monks left the house and set out for Kumano.

The woman reckoned up the day of his promised return. She could think of nothing but her love for the monk and made all sorts of preparations in anticipation. But turning homeward, he stayed away for fear of her; he took a road she did not expect him to take and thus slipped past. She waited until she was weary, but he did not come; and she went to the side of the road and questioned passing travelers. Among them was a monk who had set out from Kumano. "There was a young monk and an old one, dressed in robes of such-and-such a color"—and she described them. "Have they started homeward?" "It is three days now since those two went home," said the monk. Hearing this, she struck her hands together. "He's taken another road and fled!" she thought. In great rage she returned to her house and shut herself into her bedroom. She stayed there a little while without making a sound; and then she died. Her maidservants, who witnessed this, were weeping and wailing, when a poisonous snake forty feet long suddenly issued from her bedroom. It went out of the house and toward the road; then it slithered rapidly down the road by which pilgrims return from Kumano. People saw it and were filled with terror.

The two monks had had a head start, but someone came up to them unasked and said, "Behind you a strange thing is happening. A serpent has appeared that is forty feet long. It crosses mountains and fields and is coming rapidly closer." At this the two monks thought, "Undoubtedly, because the promise to her was broken, the mistress of that house let evil passions arise within her heart and became a poisonous snake and pursues us." Taking to their heels, they ran as fast as they could to a temple called Dōjōji and went in through the gate. "Why have you run here?" asked the monks of the temple. The two told them the story in detail and begged to be saved. The monks of the temple took counsel together; then they lowered a bell, concealed the young monk inside it, and shut the gate. The old monk hid himself in company with the monks of the temple.

After a little while, the serpent came to the temple. The gates were shut—no matter, she crossed over them and entered the compound. She went all around the halls once, twice; and when she came to the door of the bell-hall where the monk was sheltering, she rapped on it a hundred times with her tail. In the end, she smashed the leaves of the door and entered. She encircled the bell and beat upon the dragon head at its top with her tail; this lasted five or six hours. For all their fear, the monks were so amazed that they opened the doors on all four sides and gathered to watch. Tears of blood flowed from her eyes; raising her head, she licked her lips and slithered rapidly away whence she had come. Before the eyes of the monks, the great bell of the temple blazed and was burned in the poisonous hot breath of the serpent. It was too hot to come near. But they threw water on it to cool it, and when they lifted it away to look at the monk, they saw that fire had consumed him utterly. Not even his skeleton remained. All that there was, was a little ash. Upon seeing this, the old monk returned home amidst his tears.

Later, an aged monk, who was a senior monk of the temple, had a dream in which a serpent even larger than the one before came straight to him and addressed him face to face: "Do you know who I am? I am the monk who was hidden inside the bell. The evil woman became a poisonous snake; in the end, I was made her captive and became her husband. I have been reborn in this vile, filthy body and suffer measureless torment. I now hope to free myself of this pain, but my own powers are insufficient—and even though I honored the Lotus Sutra while I was alive. I thought that if only you, holy sir, would bestow on us the vastness of your mercy, I might escape this pain. I beseech you, on our account let limitless compassion arise within your heart; in purity copy the chapter of the Lotus Sutra called 'The Limitless Life of the Tathāgata.' Dedicate its merit to us two serpents and free us thereby from our torments. Except by the power of the Lotus Sutra, how are we to escape them?" Thus he spoke, and departed. The monk awoke from his dream.

When the monk pondered this afterwards, his piety was at once aroused. He himself copied out the chapter; and discarding his robe and bowl,[2] he invited a great many monks to celebrate a full day's Dharma assembly and dedicated its merit that the two serpents might be freed of their torments. Later, he dreamed that a monk and a woman, their happy faces wreathed in smiles, came to the Dōjōji and saluted him reverently. "Because you have cultivated the roots of enlightenment, we two were instantly rid of our snakes' bodies and set on the path of felicitous rebirth. The woman was reborn in the Trayastriṁśa heaven, and the monk has ascended to the Tuṣita heaven." Having spoken, they departed separately, ascending into the sky. The monk awoke from his dream.

The aged monk rejoiced deeply, and he revered all the more the miraculous power of the Lotus Sutra. In truth, the Sutra's wonder-working powers are uncanny. That the serpents cast off their serpents' bodies and were reborn afresh in the heavens is due solely to the Lotus Sutra. Everyone who witnessed this affair or heard of it was moved to belief in the Lotus Sutra and copied and chanted it. Rare, too, was the heart of the aged monk. To have done such a compassionate deed, he must in a previous life have been their wise and good friend. Now think: that evil woman's passion for the young monk must also have come from a bond formed in a previous life.

You see, therefore, the strength of the evil in the female heart. It is for this reason that the Buddha strictly forbids approaching women. Know this, and avoid them. So the tale's been told, and so it's been handed down.

Notes to Story 3

1. Deity of Kumano: literally, "provisional manifestation of Kumano." The deity in question is a Shinto deity, and "provisional manifestation" (*gongen*) refers to the idea, widespread in the middle ages, that the Shinto *kami* are manifestations of the Buddhas. Pilgrimages to Kumano, in the Kii peninsula (modern Wakayama prefecture), had been popular among all classes of society since the early tenth century. To have sexual relations with the woman would be not only a violation of the monk's Buddhist vows but a defilement, and thus highly offensive, in the eyes of the Shinto deity. The paper strips (*mitegura*, long strips of paper attached to either side of a pole) and lamps, in the passage below, are characteristic offerings at Shinto shrines.

2. In other words, at the cost of his last earthly possessions.

5. ABOUT A MAN WHO COPIED THE LOTUS SUTRA TO SAVE THE SOUL OF A FOX

AT A TIME NOW PAST, there was a fine-looking young man. Who he was, I do not know, but he must have been some nobleman's attendant. On his way back from somewhere or other, he was going past the place where Shujaku Road runs into Second Avenue. As he crossed in front of Shujaku gate[1] he saw standing in the Avenue a woman of seventeen or eighteen, flawlessly beautiful, wearing layer upon layer of fine robes. It was impossible to pass her by, and he went up to her and took her hand.

He drew her aside to a secluded spot within the gate, and there they sat, the two of them, chatting idly and intimately. He said to her, "That we should meet in this way must have been predestined. I want you to love me as I love you. Dearest, do as I desire. I ask because I love you so."

"I should like to do as you ask," said the woman. "I should like to yield to your desires; but if I do, without a doubt I shall lose my life."

The man did not understand what she was trying to say. "She's just making excuses," he thought and tried forcibly to embrace her. The woman wept piteously and said, "You're a respectable man, with a position; I suppose you've a house and a wife and children. For you this is nothing but a fleeting affair, while I will have to die in your stead — and all for a few moments' pleasure." In such terms she protested, but in the end she yielded.

The sun set, and soon it was night. He rented a small house in the neighborhood and took her there. They lay together, and afterwards the whole night through they exchanged eternal vows of love. At daybreak, as she was about to go, the woman said, "Without a doubt I shall lose my life in your stead. Therefore copy the Lotus Sutra and dedicate it to me, to ease me in the life to come." The man said, "Men and women make love every day. Why should you die of it? If you do die, of course I'll copy the Lotus Sutra for you."

The woman said, "Dearest, if you want to see whether I speak the truth, tomorrow morning go look by the Butokuden.[2] And as a sign —" She took the fan he had been carrying and parted from him in tears. The man went home; he believed none of it.

The next day he began to wonder if there might not be some truth in her words and decided to take a look. He went to the Butokuden, and as he walked around it a white-haired old woman came out, tears streaming down her face. "Who are you?" he asked, "and why are you weeping so?" The crone replied, "Sir, I am the mother of the person whom you saw last night at the

Shujaku gate. Alas! she is already dead. I have been waiting here to inform you. There lies her corpse." She pointed a finger and vanished. "That's strange," thought the man, and he went over to look. Within the hall a fox lay dead, its face covered with a fan. This fan was the one taken from him the night before. Now at last he understood. "Why, this fox is the woman I met last night! I have had intercourse with a fox!"[3] Deeply moved, overcome with the strangeness of it all, he returned home.

Beginning that very day, working each day for seven days, he copied the Lotus Sutra in its entirety and dedicated it to the welfare of the woman's soul. Even before the seven days were ended he reencountered the woman in a dream. She wore clothes and ornaments as befitted a goddess, and a great throng of women similarly adorned surrounded her. She said to him, "Thanks to you, I have been saved; by your copying the Lotus Sutra on my behalf, my sins have been extinguished for aeon upon aeon, and now I have been reborn in the Trayastriṁśa heaven. My gratitude to you is boundless; however many rebirths we may pass through, I shall never forget what I owe you," and she ascended into the sky as wondrous music filled the air. The man awoke from his dream. He was filled with reverence, and, deeply moved, he dedicated the Lotus Sutra with even more fervent faith.

That man had a rare heart. Even though it was the woman's dying injunction, would he otherwise so assiduously have honored his promise to serve her soul's welfare? Surely he must have been her wise and good friend in a previous life. So the tale's been told, and so it's been handed down.

Notes to Story 5

1. Shujaku (or Suzaku) gate was the principal gate of the imperial palace and was at the northern end of Shujaku Road; Second Avenue was the southern border of the enclosure.

2. A pavilion within the imperial enclosure from which the emperor watched horse-racing and archery contests.

3. The original readers of the story would have already suspected that this was the case when the woman protested that she would have to die in place of her lover. A human being who has sexual relations with a fox ordinarily will die.

Chapter Fifteen

28. HOW A PRIEST OF CHINZEI WHO ATE CARRION WAS REBORN IN PARADISE

AT A TIME NOW PAST, there was a monk who exerted himself in practicing the Way of the Buddha. He went everywhere throughout the more than sixty provinces of Japan, worshipped at every holy place, and in the course of his travels came to Chinzei.[1] While he was touring the provinces of that island on foot, he suddenly lost his way in the mountains and came to an area that was completely uninhabited. "If only I could manage to come out at a village!" he thought in his distress, but days passed and he found no way out of the wilderness.

Just by chance he caught sight of a spot in the mountains where there was a single grass hut. Much relieved, he went to the door and asked if he could spend the night. A woman came out of the hut and said, "Sir, this is not a suitable place for lodgers." The monk said, "In the course of a pilgrimage I have lost my way in the mountains. I am exhausted and have no strength to go on. By good fortune I came here. Even if there should be some difficulty, please give me lodging." The woman said, "Since you insist, sir, you may stay for this one night." Highly pleased, the monk went into the hut. The woman took out a clean mat and spread it for the monk to sit on; she prepared pure food for him, and he ate it all.

After nightfall, a man came with something on his back. He went into the hut and set down the thing he had been carrying. The traveler saw that he was a priest[2] — but with hair three or four inches long, dressed in rags. His appearance was horrifying: he was too filthy to come near. Under the eyes of the monk, he questioned the woman: "Who is our visitor?" She replied, "He is a pilgrim who has lost his way. He will stay here just for tonight." The priest said, "It is five or six years now since anyone of his sort has been seen here. This is entirely unexpected." He ate what he had carried in; it was the flesh of oxen and horses. Seeing him, the monk thought, "What an ill place I have come to! This is the house of carrion-eaters." But it was night, he had nowhere else to go, and so he stayed where he was. The stench of the meat filled the narrow room, filthy and disagreeable beyond measure.

He lay awake. An hour or two past midnight he heard the priest get up, wash himself in warm water, put on clothing that had been set apart, and go out the hut toward the back. "What can he be up to?" thought the monk, and he secretly stationed himself to listen. To his astonishment, there behind the hut was a hall for sacred images, no more than six feet deep. The priest went in, lit the altar lamps, and placed incense in front of the Buddha. First he recited the Lotus Confessional;[3] then he performed a reading of the entire Lotus Sutra; and then, after reverently saluting the image, he intoned the invocation to Amida. His voice was of matchless nobility.

At dawn he went out of the image hall and encountered the monk. He told his story, and this is what he said: "I, Jōson, disciple of the Buddha, am stupid and unenlightened. Even though I was born in a human body and have become a priest, I shamelessly break the commandments, and when I die I shall fall into an evil path. Nor am I one who will enjoy prosperity in this present life. I dearly desire to follow the path of the Buddha, but I can neither keep the rules and commandments of monastic life nor carry out the three kinds of good deeds, so that I am unable to conform to the Buddha's teaching. Born as a vulgar mortal, I sin through feeding and clothing myself. Suppose I got some patron—with what merit would I repay his kindness? And so, I inevitably sin in everything. For this reason, I seek out food that ordinary people won't even look at and prolong my existence while I long for the Buddha path. This food I speak of is the flesh of oxen and horses. But now, through some karmic bond from a previous life, you have come here. I speak to you in thankfulness and joy. A few years will pass, and then, on a certain day of a certain month in a certain year"—and he named them—"I shall abandon this mortal realm and be reborn in paradise."

Upon hearing this, the monk thought, "He seemed a base fellow, a beggar or worse, but in fact he is a noble sage." And with earnest and repeated vows to return, he left that place and went to a village.

Some years passed, and the promised time arrived. The monk went to that place to learn whether what the other had foretold was truth or lie. Jōson saw him coming and rejoiced mightily. Jōson said, "This very night I shall cast off this body and be reborn in paradise. I gave up eating meat three or four months ago." He shaved his head, bathed, and put on pure garments. Moreover, the woman whom the traveler had seen had become a nun. Soon it was night. As before, the monk stayed in the hut and watched; and as he did so, both Jōson and the nun entered the Buddha-image hall. All night long he heard them together chant the invocation to Amida. At daybreak a great light shone within the hut. Even as the monk saw this and marveled, a wondrous music sounded in the air. At length, the radiance departed westward. All the while, an indescribable fragrance filled the hut. When it was fully daylight, the monk entered the image hall. Both Jōson and the nun were dead. Their hands were clasped in prayer, and they were seated as for meditation, facing west.

Seeing them, the monk shed copious tears and saluted reverently. He did not leave this place but settled in the hut to practice the Dharma of the Buddha. Whenever anyone in the province chanced to hear of what had happened in that spot, he would go there to establish a karmic bond. What became of the place afterwards, I don't know.

One of the people of the province who had gone there told the story. "A queer tale, isn't it!" he said, and others heard it and passed it on. So the tale's been told, and so it's been handed down.

Notes to Story 28

1. Old name for Kyushu.

2. *Hōshi*. The visitor is a *sō*, a word which I have routinely translated as "monk." *Hōshi* can be used synonymously with *sō*; or it can be used for a wide variety of adepts and lay devotees in religious garb. In this story I have translated *hōshi* as "priest," simply as an aid in distinguishing the two principal actors.

3. A rite practiced in the Tendai school, in which the devotee chants the Lotus Sutra and confesses and repents the sins of the six senses.

Chapter Sixteen

17. HOW KAYA NO YOSHIFUJI, OF BITCHŪ PROVINCE, BECAME THE HUSBAND OF A FOX AND WAS SAVED BY KANNON

AT A TIME NOW PAST, in the village of Ashimori in Kaya District of Bitchū Province, there lived a man named Kaya no Yoshifuji. His household had gotten rich through the trade in coins.[1] He had a weakness for women and was prey to lustful thoughts.

Now, in autumn of the eighth year of Kanpei,[2] while his wife was away in the capital and he, left by himself in his household, was a temporary widower, he went out for a stroll just at nightfall and suddenly caught sight of a beautiful young woman. She was someone he had never seen before. His lustful feelings were aroused, but the woman looked as though she would flee if he tried to touch her. He went up to her and took her by the hand. "Who are you?" he asked. She was brilliantly dressed, but she said, "I'm no one." How charming she looked as she said that! "Come to my house," said Yoshifuji. "That would be unseemly," she said, and tried to draw away. "Where do you live, then?" said Yoshifuji; "I'll go with you." "Just over there," she said, walking on. Yoshifuji walked with her, holding her hand.

Close by, there was a handsome house; inside, too, it was sumptuously furnished. "Odd," thought Yoshifuji, "I never knew there was anything like this here." Within, there was a great clamor, as men and women, persons of every degree, together cried, "Her Ladyship's come!" "This must be the daughter of the house," Yoshifuji thought, delightedly, and that night he slept with her.

The next morning a man who was evidently the master of the house appeared. "Congratulations," he said to Yoshifuji, "this bond was predestined! Now you must stay with us." Yoshifuji was treated very hospitably. He became utterly attached to the woman; they vowed eternal love, and waking and sleeping he spent all his time with her. He never wondered how his house and children might be faring.

In his own home, when he had not reappeared after nightfall, people thought, "Maybe he's crawling around somewhere in secret, in his usual way." But when it was quite dark and he still had not reappeared, there were some who took it amiss. "What a madman he is! Have the servants look for him." The night was more than half gone, but though they searched the neighborhood, he was not to be found. Could he have gone on a journey? But his clothing was still there; he had disappeared wearing only a light jacket. Day broke and the uproar continued. They looked everywhere that he might have gone but found absolutely nothing. "If he were a young man with unsettled ideas, he might have gone off suddenly to become a monk. But at his age? It's a very strange prank — if it is one." Meanwhile, where Yoshifuji was living, the years passed. His wife was pregnant, and after nine months she gave birth, without complications, to a son, so that he became even more deeply attached to her. It seemed to him indeed that time was passing swiftly; everything in his life was just as he desired it.

In his own home, after he disappeared, he was sought for, but without success. His older brother, the Senior Officer Toyonaka, his younger brothers, the Supervisor Toyokage and Toyotsune, who was priest of the Kibitsuhiko shrine, and Yoshifuji's only son, Tadasada, were all affluent men. In their mutual grief, they decided to try at least to discover his corpse. Good resolves arose in them, and they felled a *kae* tree to make an image of the eleven-headed Kannon. The statue they made was the same height as Yoshifuji. They petitioned it: "At least let us see his corpse," they pleaded. Moreover, from the day on which he disappeared, they began invocations of the Buddha and sutra readings for the welfare of his soul in the next world.

A layman who walked with a staff came suddenly to the house where Yoshifuji was now living. At the sight of him, the whole household, from the master on down, fell into utter terror and fled. The layman jabbed Yoshifuji in the back with his staff, forcing him out through a narrow passageway. At twilight on the thirteenth day after Yoshifuji's disappearance, his people were mourning him. "What a strange way he disappeared! And it was just about this time of night, wasn't it?" they were saying to each other, when from underneath the storehouse in front of them a strange, black, monkey-like creature crawled out on all fours. "What's this, what's this!" They crowded in to look at it. "It's me," said the thing—and the voice was Yoshifuji's. His son, Tadasada, thought it uncanny, but since it was so obviously his father's voice, he dropped to the ground and pulled him up. "What happened to you?" he said. Yoshifuji said, "It was while I was a widower and by myself. All the time I kept thinking how much I wanted to have a woman.[3] And then, unexpectedly, I became the son-in-law of a high-ranking gentleman. During the years I've lived in his household I've gotten a son. He's a beautiful child. I held him in my arms day and night and wouldn't let go of him ever. I'm going to make him my heir. You, Tadasada, I'll make my second son. That's to show my regard for his mother's high rank." Tadasada heard this and said, "Where is your young son, sir?" "Over there," said Yoshifuji, and pointed to the storehouse.

Tadasada and all the rest of the company were dumbfounded. They saw that Yoshifuji had the appearance of a man emaciated by severe illness; and they saw that he had on the clothes that he was wearing when he disappeared. They had a servant look under the floor of the storehouse. A lot of foxes were there, and they scattered and fled. That was the place where Yoshifuji had lain. When they saw this they understood it all: Yoshifuji had been tricked by a fox and had become her husband and was no longer in his right mind. They immediately summoned an eminent monk to pray for him and called in a yin-yang master to exorcise the evil influences; and they had Yoshifuji bathed repeatedly. But whatever they tried, he still bore no resemblance to his former self. Afterwards, little by little, he returned to his senses; how ashamed he must have been, and how queer he must have felt. Yoshifuji had been under the storehouse for thirteen days, but to him it had seemed thirteen years. Moreover, the beams under the storehouse were only four or five inches above the ground; to Yoshifuji they had seemed high and broad. He had thought himself in a great house that one went in and out of freely. It was all because of the magic power of the spirit-foxes. As for the layman who entered and struck about with his cane, he was a transformation of the Kannon that had been made and dedicated to Yoshifuji's welfare.

This shows why everyone should invoke and meditate on Kannon. Yoshifuji lived more than ten years without illness and died in his sixty-first year.

This story was told to the Imperial Adviser Miyoshi no Kiyotsura[4] when he was governor of Bitchū. So the tale's been told, and so it's been handed down.

<hr>

Notes to Story 17

1. I.e., in coins imported from China.

2. The year 896.

3. Thus — by having sexual longings — making himself an easy victim for foxes, as the Japanese readers would have recognized. More subtle clues, which the original readers would have been expected to spot: when the young woman, asked her name, says "I'm no one"; when the worried relatives, wondering if he isn't off on a secret love affair, suggest jocosely (and all too accurately) that he may be "crawling" about somewhere.

4. Miyoshi Kiyotsura (or Kiyoyuki, 847–918) was, among other things, a scholar of Chinese. Among his numerous works is a collection of anecdotes of the supernatural. This is one of the few places in which the *Konjaku* compiler may be explicitly acknowledging his immediate source.

20. HOW TRAVELERS FROM CHINZEI, THROUGH KANNON'S AID, ESCAPED BEING KILLED BY BANDITS

AT A TIME NOW PAST, there was a Senior Assistant Commissioner of the Dazaifu[1] [whose name is no longer known]. He had numerous progeny, the youngest of them a boy barely in his twentieth year. This son was handsome, smart, and prudent, and though it was not a military house, he was physically strong and had exceptional courage. His parents loved him dearly, and so they had taken him along with them when they went to Chinzei. The Junior Assistant Commissioner at that time was a governor of Chikuzen[2] [whose name is no longer known], and he had a daughter. She was lovely to look at and had a gentle disposition, and she was not yet in her twentieth year. Her parents doted on her, and so they had brought her with them when they went to Chikuzen.

The Senior Assistant Commissioner urged that his son be united with the Junior Assistant Commissioner's daughter. The governor could hardly refuse his chief, and on an auspicious day the two young people were married. Man and wife soon formed a profound bond of love. The man had from before had aspirations toward a government post. About to set out for the capital, he found it hard to be separated from his wife even for a short time. "Let us go together," he said, and she agreed to accompany him. Thinking the sea route too precarious, he made haste by land. With him there were some twenty retainers whom he had especially selected, many men on foot, and numerous laden horses.

They traveled night and day. A little past four one afternoon they were passing through Inamino in Harima Province. It was the twelfth month; a strong wind was blowing, and there was a light snowfall. From the north, where mountains lay, a priest[3] came riding. He approached and dismounted before them, and they saw that he was past fifty, stout, and prosperous-looking. He wore a gown of red damask and purple laced trousers; on his feet were straw snow-boots. The whip he carried was finely lacquered, and the horse he rode bore a saddle inlaid with mother-of-pearl. He spoke reverentially: "For many years I have had the honor to be the vassal of his lordship the Governor of Chikuzen. I happened to get wind of your journey to the capital and have come to invite you to rest your horses at my humble dwelling." His manner was all that politeness could require. The retainers all dismounted, and their master reined in his horse. "I have urgent business in the capital," he said, "and am traveling night and day. I must decline, but since you are so eager to entertain us, I will certainly come to you on my way back next year." The monk persisted, and before they could decently get away the sun had sunk to the rim of the mountains. "He insists so," said the retainers. "All right," said the master, and they followed the priest. He led the way in high good humor.

"We're almost there," the priest said, but they went on for two or three more miles. Nestled at the foot of the mountains was a cluster of buildings surrounded by a high mud and timber wall.

They went in. Husband and wife were shown into a building which was in the south of the compound and which they took to be the main living quarters. A variety of refreshment was placed before them. The quarters for attendants were far away. There amidst endless hubbub the retainers were richly feasted and their horses were given fodder. Husband and wife, alone with just a maid or two, loosened their clothes and lay down. The tables were full of delicacies, and there was wine, but weary and anxious, they paid no heed. The maids ate and drank heartily and lay down to sleep. Husband and wife lay awake with their cares, talking of this and that, renewing their vows of love. "What will happen on this journey? I've a feeling of foreboding." The night gradually deepened.

From the interior of the house came the sound of footsteps. Something wasn't right, the man thought. The footsteps came nearer and a door was slid open behind his bed. "Who's that!" he thought and leaped up; someone grabbed him by the hair and dragged him away. Strong though he was, the attack was so sudden that he was carried away before he quite knew what was happening, and he was unable even to lay hands on the sword by his pillow. His captor kicked open the shutters and thrust him outside. "Kaneomaro, are you there? Follow the usual procedure with care." "Yes, sir," replied a dreadful voice, and the man was taken by the neck and hustled along. A mud and timber wall had been thrown up around a corner of the compound; a door within it gave entrance to a pit some thirty feet deep, dug in the shape of a well. In the floor sharpened stakes had been planted upright without a space between. For years, travelers like him, on their way to or from the capital, had been lured inside the compound and given intoxicating wine that made them lie as though dead for a whole day and night. The masters were thrown into this pit and impaled; meanwhile, their dead-drunk attendants were stripped of their gear and clothing. Those among them who were to be killed were killed, while those who were to be left alive were spared and pressed into service. This was the place to which the man had come unwittingly.

Kaneomaro dragged him along to the pit. Opening the door, Kaneomaro stood on the near side of it and pushed him; but the man caught hold of one of the door-posts and stood fast. Kaneomaro went to the pit side of the doorway to try to pull him in.

There was a slight downward slope: the man dodged and gave Kaneomaro a violent shove, and the ruffian fell head over heels into the pit. The man shut the door and crept under the veranda. He crouched there, thinking. What was he to do? He would have liked to go rouse his retainers, but they were dead drunk; moreover, a moat lay between, and the bridge was drawn.

He stole under the floor of the main room and listened. The priest had come to his wife and was saying, "You seem to think me not to your liking, but I saw your face this afternoon when the wind blew your veil open and I can think of nothing but you. Excuse my impertinence," and he lay down in bed beside her. She, however, said, "On this journey I've honored a vow I once made to be abstinent for a hundred days. Now I have only three days left. If you can wait, wait till the three days are over, and then I will do as you say." "Madam, the act I shall have you perform will be far more meritorious," said the priest. But the woman said, "The man I relied on has vanished before my eyes. Now I am entirely in your hands and cannot refuse you. You mustn't be hasty." She would not be intimate with him, and the monk went back into the interior of the house, saying, "Well, after all, it's only reasonable."

The woman was thinking, "That man of mine would never die so ignominiously"—meanwhile, under the floor, her husband listened in bitter rage. There was a large hole in the floorboards in front of the spot where she was sitting, and when he saw it he took a sliver of wood and thrust it through. "I was right!" she thought, catching sight of the sliver, and tugged it and wiggled it. "She has understood!" he thought. The priest came back repeatedly and tried to persuade her, but she made one excuse after another and would not listen to him, so that he went away again.

The woman then silently opened the shutters, and the man came out from under the floor and entered the room. First they wept together, shedding endless tears. "If we die, let us die together," they thought. "What about my sword?" the man asked. "When you were dragged away I hid it under a mat," she replied, and pulled it out. The man rejoiced, made her put on a single robe, and sword in hand stole toward the attendants' quarters in the north. He espied a long fire pit with seven or eight chopping blocks beside it. The priest's men were there in force, enjoying a disorderly feast, their bows, quivers, armor and helmets, swords and daggers laid out beside them. The priest himself had been feeding from silver vessels on a pair of tables before him; slumped against an armrest, he was asleep in his seat amidst the leavings.

Then the man sent up a silent prayer: "O Kannon of Hatsuse, Holy Bodhisattva, save me! Let me see my father and mother once again!" It occurred to him: "This priest is asleep and off his guard. I'll charge him and cut off his head. We'll die together. I can't escape anyway." He stole up to the priest, took aim at his drooping neck, and struck with all his might. The priest yelled, raised his hands, and fell over. He struck again and again, and the priest died.

The men before him were a goodly number, but truly our man was aided by Kannon, for they thought that a great multitude had burst upon them and killed their master. Moreover, they had no wish to fight: they themselves had all been the priest's captives. Not one thought to raise a hand to save him; and how much less did they care to put up a fight now that he was dead. Their strength left them, and from every mouth arose "It's not our fault. We were followers of so-and-so and made to serve here against our will." The man drove them into suitable enclosures, all the while behaving as though he had an ample escort, and awaited the dawn with an uneasy heart. At dawn he called out his own retainers. They emerged from their quarters as though dreaming, rubbing their eyes, still half drunk. But when they heard what had happened, they became sober.

They went to open the door through which their master had almost fallen. They saw the floor of the deep pit, and the sharpened bamboo stakes planted in it without a space between, and many corpses, old and new, of those who had died on them. The "Kaneomaro" of the preceding night was a tall, skinny youth wearing a single coarse robe; he had been impaled with his clogs on and, not quite dead yet, was still squirming. "This must be what hell is like," they thought.

The men who had been in this house the night before were called out, and all came. As one, they avowed that for years they had served against their will, and so they were not punished. A messenger was sent to the capital with a report. The Emperor heard of it and exclaimed in admiration of the splendid deed. When the man arrived in the capital he was given an official post. He lived with his wife in such prosperity as anyone might wish;

how tears and laughter mingled when they spoke of old times! As for the robber priest and those who must have been his associates, nothing more is known of them.

People who are smart and prudent sometimes do such lucky deeds. Nevertheless, you who hear this tale should think twice before going into unfamiliar places.

And another thing: it was solely through Kannon's help that this man was saved. Though Kannon would never wish to kill a man, how evil he must have thought one who himself had killed so many! And so, killing an evil man is the act of a bodhisattva. So the tale's been told, and so it's been handed down.

Notes to Story 20

1. Dazaifu was the government headquarters in Kyushu, having control over Kyushu and neighboring islands.

2. Chikuzen was a province within Kyushu; the governor held dual office and was the Senior Assistant Commissioner's subordinate.

3. *Hōshi:* see 15:28, note 2.

32. HOW AN INVISIBLE MAN REGAINED CORPOREAL FORM THROUGH KANNON'S AID

AT A TIME NOW PAST — when it was I do not know — there lived in the capital a young, low-ranking samurai. He went regularly to the Rokkakudō[1] and worshipped there earnestly.

On the last day of the twelfth month[2] it happened that at nightfall he went to the house of a friend. He set out for home after it was quite dark and went west down First Avenue. As he was crossing the bridge over Horikawa[3] he saw ahead of him a great many men carrying lighted torches. "It must be some high nobleman," he thought and hurried under the bridge. He waited in its shadow as the torch-bearers came toward him and passed over it eastward. He raised his eyes for a quiet look — and what should he see but that it was not men at all but a procession of dreadful oni! Some had one eye; some had horns; some had extra hands; and some had only one foot and hopped. At the sight, the man felt as though he were no longer alive; his mind went numb and he just stood there as the oni went by. They had all gone past except for one last, and *he* said, "There are signs of a man here." "We can't see any," some said. "Catch him and bring him here," said yet others.

"It's all over with me," the man thought. One of the oni ran and grabbed him and pulled him up. The others said, "This man's offense is not serious. Let him go." Four or five of them spat on him, and then they all went past.

The man was glad that he hadn't been killed. He felt funny and his head hurt, but he pulled himself together. "I'll go straight home and tell my wife about it," he thought. He hurried home, but once he was indoors his wife and children said not a word to him although they were looking right at him; nor did they answer when he addressed them. The man thought this strange and went up close to them, but even though he was standing beside them they had no idea he was there. Now he understood. "So that's it! When the oni spat on me my body disappeared!" His distress was boundless. He saw other people just as before and heard them talk as clearly as ever, but other people did not see him or hear his voice. He took food to eat which his family had set out, and none of them knew it. Thus he passed the night; at dawn his wife and children were saying that they were sure he had been murdered the night before.

Days passed—and what was he to do? With no other remedy, he went to the Rokkakudō and went into retreat there. "Kannon, save me!" he prayed. "For many years now I have worshipped you and put my trust in you; as proof of it let me regain my original corporeal form." He ate the food of others who were in retreat there and took rice from their offerings, but none of the people beside him were aware of it.

Thus he spent twice seven days. One night shortly before dawn he had a dream. A venerable monk appeared near the curtains of the sacred image and came to his side. The monk said, "Leave this place as soon as it is morning and do as the first person you meet tells you to." At this, the man awoke.

At dawn he left the temple. At the foot of the gate he met a herdboy whose appearance was fearsome in the extreme, leading a great ox. The boy looked at him and said, "Well, sir, you're to come along with me." The man was overjoyed at being spoken to, for he thought, "I have become visible again," and, trusting in his dream, followed the boy happily. They walked westward for about two-thirds of a mile and came to a large gabled gate, which was shut fast. The boy tied his ox to it and started to slip through a space between the doors too narrow for a human being to enter. He tugged at the man. "Come in with me," he said. "How on earth can I get through that?" said the man. "Never mind," said the boy, "just go in" — and taking the man's hand, he pulled him in along with him. The man saw that they were within the walls of a great, thronging mansion.

The boy took him up onto the veranda floor and straight inside. Not a person spoke up to challenge them. They went into the innermost recesses of the house, and there the man saw a fine young lady lying sick and in pain. Her maids sat side by side behind her pillow and at her feet, nursing her. The oxboy led the man to the sick lady, made him hold a small mallet, sat him down beside her, and made him strike her head and hips, so that she shook her head in agony. "This illness will be the end of her," her parents said, and they wept. As the man looked on, they read sutras, and also they sent for [a certain]⁴ worthy exorcist. Soon the priest arrived. Sitting close to the sick girl, he intoned the Heart Sutra. The man felt boundless veneration. His hair stood on end, and a chill went through his body. But no sooner did the oxboy catch sight of the priest than he, for his part, ran out of the house at full speed.

The priest read a dharani of Fudō's realm of fire.⁵ When he pronounced the formula and made mystic signs over the patient, the man's clothing caught fire. It burned and burned, and as it burned he screamed. At that moment he became fully visible. Everyone in the household, from the parents down to the maids, saw to their amazement a man obviously of very lowly station sitting next to the sufferer. Before anything else, they took hold of him and dragged him away. "What is this?" they demanded, and he told them what had happened, from the very beginning. "What a queer business!" they thought. But then it turned out that when the man had become visible the lady had recovered: it was as though her illness had been simply wiped away. The joy of the household was unbounded. The exorcist then said: "Do not blame this man, for he has benefited from the favor of the Kannon of Rokkakudō. Release him at once." And so they let him go free.

The man went home and told his story, and his wife was glad and thought how uncanny it all was. The oxboy was in fact the attendant of a deity. He had afflicted the lady because someone had persuaded him to.

Neither the lady nor the man was ever ill afterward; this resulted from the miraculous power of the realm of fire dharani.

Among the benefits with which Kannon favors his worshippers are marvels of this sort. So the tale's been told, and so it's been handed down.

Notes to Story 32

1. A hall in the Chōhōji, in Kyoto, in which a celebrated image of Kannon was enshrined.

2. In ancient times the spirits of the dead were thought to return on this night. There is a reference to this belief in *Tsurezuregusa;* the author complains that the custom of paying homage to them has lapsed in the capital but says that it is still preserved in the provinces. See Donald Keene, trans., *Essays in Idleness* (New York and London: Columbia University Press, 1967), pp. 20–21.

3. First Avenue was the northern boundary of Kyoto; Horikawa was to the west.

4. Bracketed words bridge a lacuna; literally, "a worthy exorcist called ———."

5. Through chanting, mystic gestures, and meditation on Fudō, the adept produced a magic fire to drive out demons. The passage that follows may be unique in literature in describing an exorcism essentially from the point of view of the supernatural being who is exorcised.

Chapter Seventeen

1. ABOUT A MONK WHO PRAYED TO MEET A MANIFESTATION OF THE BODHISATTVA JIZŌ

AT A TIME NOW PAST, in the western part of the capital, there lived a monk. He was pious, and he earnestly practiced the Way of the Buddha. Among his devotions was for many years the worship of Jizō. He prayed: "May I in this present life meet Jizō in the flesh, and may I not fail to receive his welcome into paradise when I die." On this account he went from province to province, seeking for the place where Jizō would perform his miracle. People who heard what was on his mind made fun of him. "What a stupid wish!" they said. "How could you ever hope to meet a real, live Jizō?"

But he would not give up, and he went to one province after another, and came to Hitachi. As he walked about aimlessly the sun set, and he took lodging at a wretched peasant hut. In this house there was a single old woman and also an oxboy, a lad in his fifteenth or sixteenth year. As he was watching, someone came and called the boy outside; afterwards he heard the boy scream and weep. Soon the boy came back in, still weeping. "Why is he crying?" the monk asked the old woman. "It's because he tends the master's ox. He's constantly punished; that's why he weeps. His father died when he was very young, and he has no one to look after him. But since he was born on the twenty-fourth day of the month, he is named Jizōmaro."

The monk thought to himself that there was something strange about what he was hearing. "Can it be?" he wondered — "can it be that this boy is Jizō in human form, responding to my prayers of many years? The compassionate vows of the bodhisattvas are indeed marvelous beyond the comprehension of ordinary mortals." He found it hard to understand and meditated all the more fervently on Jizō. He lay sleepless all night, and just as he was thinking that it must be some hours past midnight, he heard the boy sit up and say, "These past years I have been employed by my present master and have had to endure his beatings, but now that I have had the honor of meeting the monk who is lodging with us I shall go elsewhere." Without seeming to go out, he vanished. The monk was astounded. "What was that the boy said?" he asked the old woman, whereupon she too, without seeming to go out, vanished.

The monk then knew that it had in truth been a manifestation of Jizō. He shouted at the top of his voice, but neither the woman nor the boy was seen again. After daybreak he went among the people of the village and told them amidst tears how the old woman and the boy had disappeared. "For many years I have worshipped Jizō and prayed that I might meet him in human form. Now my prayers have been answered. I have met Jizō in the flesh. What a miracle!" Tears streamed from the eyes of the villagers, and all were overcome with awe.

This shows that, difficult though it is, anyone can see Jizō if he prays with true faith. He whose prayers are perfunctory will never meet him. The monk went up to the capital and told his story there, and those who heard it repeated it. So the tale's been told, and so it's been handed down.

2. HOW KI NO MOCHIKATA WORSHIPPED JIZŌ AND BENEFITED FROM HIS FAVOR

AT A TIME NOW PAST, there was a former governor of Owari [whose name is no longer known].[1] After many years of official service, he renounced secular life and took the name of lay-monk. Among his followers there was a man of warlike temperament named Musashi no Suke Ki no Mochikata. Mochikata was bold and fierce and unrestrainedly perverse in mind, with not a single good impulse. Something must have happened, however, for suddenly he was firmly aroused to piety. He had especial faith in the Bodhisattva Jizō. On the twenty-fourth day of each month he abstained from wine and meat, kept away from women, and devoted himself entirely to meditating on Jizō. He also recited the name of Amida day and night. In addition, he regularly observed the monks' precept of eating only before noon.

However, Mochikata had a violent temper, and if by chance

something was said that displeased him, his anger would blaze like fire. People who witnessed such incidents scolded and laughed at him and called him incorrigible. But even as his temper was rising he would meditate on Jizō and unflaggingly recite the name of Amida.

Now in those days there was an Amida *hijiri*[2] who traveled night and day exhorting people to recite the invocation to Amida. This holy man dreamed that he met a golden Jizō. Jizō addressed him. "Tomorrow at dawn," he said, "you will know me without fail in the first person you see as you walk down that lane." The holy man awoke, his heart filled with joy to think that he would meet a manifestation of Jizō. At dawn the next morning, as he was going down that certain lane to preach, a layman came toward him. "Who are you?" asked the holy man. "I am Ki no Mochikata," said the layman. Hearing this, the holy man repeatedly made obeisance to Mochikata. Tears streaming down his face, shaken and awed, the holy man said, "Thanks to the good karma from my previous lives, I have met the Bodhisattva Jizō. I pray you, show me the Way."

Mochikata was astounded. "I am an evil man with perverse views. Why, sir, do you weep and bow to me?" The holy man said amidst tears, "Last night I dreamed that I met a golden Jizō, who told me, 'Tomorrow at dawn you will know me without fail in the first person you meet as you walk down this lane.' Trusting profoundly in my dream, I have met you, sir. I know for certain that you are Jizō in human form." At these words Mochikata thought to himself, "For many years now I have been meditating on Jizō. Is it possible that Jizō is giving me a sign?" and he parted from the holy man. Afterwards, Mochikata's faith was aroused even more, and he devoted himself without restraint to his meditation on Jizō.

In his declining years Mochikata finally renounced secular life and entered religion. More than ten years passed; though he felt some illness, he had no pain. His faith was firm; facing west he chanted Amida's name and meditated on the name of Jizō. Thus he passed away.

All those who witnessed this or heard of it, monks and laymen, men and women alike, shed reverent tears. So the tale's been told, and so it's been handed down.

Notes to Story 2

1. Literally, a man named——no——. In *Jizō bosatsu reigenki,* he appears simply as "a former governor of Owari." See Dykstra, "Jizō," pp. 192–193. The intention, here unfulfilled, of presenting more precise detail than the sources provide is characteristic of *Konjaku.*

2. Followers of Kūya (903–972; the name is also read Kōya), who traveled among the people, urging them to recite Amida's name.

44. HOW A MONK THROUGH BISHAMONTEN'S AID BEGOT GOLD AND OBTAINED A MEANS OF SUPPORT

AT A TIME NOW PAST, there was a monk of Mount Hiei [of which cloister is no longer known].[1] Although he was a scholar of great eminence, he was desperately poor and, lacking a powerful patron, was unable to obtain a residence on the Mountain. He went down to the capital and settled in a cloister called the Urin'in. Without parents or relations or anyone to put in a word for him, he had no dependable means of support. For many years he had been going to Kuramadera to pray to Bishamonten[2] to relieve him.

Now on the twentieth day of the ninth month he went to Kuramadera. On his return journey the sun set while he was in the neighborhood of the Izumo road. A single shabby-looking acolyte was his companion. As the moon was very bright, he made haste toward his home. Just as he was about to turn into one of the lanes north of First Avenue, he was joined by a handsome lad in his seventeenth or eighteenth year, faultlessly dressed in a loosely belted white robe. "He must be a temple boy out for a stroll," the monk thought, "but why isn't his master with him? How strange!"

The boy drew near to him and said, "Where are you going, sir?"

"To the Urin'in," replied the monk.

"Let me go with you, sir," said the boy.

"Young man," said the monk, "I don't know who you are.

Wouldn't that be irresponsible of me? Surely you're on your way somewhere, to your master, or to your parents' house. You say 'Let me go with you' — now, I'd be glad to have you, but think of the unpleasantness later on."

"You're right, sir," said the boy, "but I've had a difference with the monk who's been my friend all these years, and for the last ten days I've wandered around homeless. My parents died when I was little. I thought that if there's someone who'll be nice to me I'll stay with him wherever he goes."

"I'm glad of that!" said the monk. "Even if there's ugly talk afterwards, I shan't have committed a sin. But all the same, there's no one in my rooms except a lowly acolyte. I'm afraid you'll be much too bored." They chatted as they walked.

The boy was so extraordinarily beautiful that he quite captured the monk's heart. "Come what may, I'll take him with me," the monk thought, and they went together to his chamber in the Urin'in. Lighting a lamp, the monk examined the boy: his complexion was white and his face plump; he was refined in every way and utterly adorable. Seeing him, the monk was overjoyed. It was evident that the boy was of good birth. "What was your father called?" he asked, but the boy answered none of his questions. He prepared the place for sleeping more carefully than usual and put the boy to bed; he lay down next to him and they talked of one thing and another and went to sleep.

The next morning the monks in the neighboring cells all joined in admiring the boy's beauty. The monk was unwilling to have anyone see him and would not let him out even onto the veranda. On this day, after the sun had gone down, the monk drew close to him and began now to caress him familiarly. But as he did so a strange suspicion entered his mind.

He said to the boy, "Since the time of my birth, I have not touched a woman's skin except for my mother's breast, and so I don't properly know — But this is so odd! It's not at all like being in bed with a boy. I don't know why, but my heart simply melts toward you. Can it be that you're a woman? Is that so? Tell me the truth. From the moment I first saw you, I haven't felt able to part from you for an instant; and this seems even stranger and harder to understand."

The boy burst out laughing. "What if I am a woman? I suppose that wouldn't suit you."

"But I'm afraid of what people will say if I have a woman living with me," said the monk. "And what the Buddha himself will think — that I dread!"

"The Buddha will indeed be angry with you if you let your feelings be aroused," said the boy, seeming much diverted. "And people who see us will certainly know that you're keeping a boy. But suppose I am a woman: just behave as though you were talking fondly with a boy."

"So it is a woman!" the monk thought, and his fear and mortification were boundless. But desire for her suffused his entire being; she was adorable and seductive; and so, instead of putting her out after what he had heard, he took off his clothes as though unconcerned and lay down to sleep. But he was an ordinary man after all, and in the end he abandoned caution and made love to her. Afterwards, throughout the night, he reflected that even the most beautiful of boys could not be so lovable. And meanwhile the monks in the neighboring cells were saying, "Poor as he is, how ever did he get his hands on a splendid young gentleman!"

Now the "boy" began to feel not her usual self and stopped eating. The monk thought this most peculiar. "You must know that I'm pregnant," said the boy. The monk listened with an expression of dismay.

"For months I've been telling people you're a boy, but now I don't know what to do. What will I do when you bear the child?"

"Do nothing," said the boy. "Say nothing. I won't trouble you."

The months passed. The monk thought of her with a heavy heart. As her time came near, the boy became anxious and spoke piteously, crying without restraint. The monk was filled with concern. The boy said, "My belly hurts. I feel that I'm about to give birth." The monk was at his wits' end. "Don't be so distraught," said the boy. "Find me a suitable shed and spread a mat in it."

The monk did as the boy told him, laying out a mat in a storage shed. The boy was there only a short time, it seemed, and then the baby was born. The mother took off her own robe to cover the child and was lying with it in her arms; suddenly she was no longer there. Astonished and mystified, the monk approached, quietly pulled back the robe, and saw that there was no child but a large stone the size of a pillow. Fright overcame him at the weirdness of it; but in the first light of morning he saw that the stone had a yellow radiance. He examined it closely and saw that it was gold. The "boy" had disappeared; she who had once been rose up in the monk's imagination and moved him to longing. He reflected nonetheless that it had been wholly a scheme of the Bishamonten of Kuramadera to succor him. Afterwards he broke up the lump of gold and sold it bit by bit, so that in truth he became prosperous in all things.

Gold used to be called *kigane,* "yellow metal"; it must be since this that it's been called *kogane,* "child metal."

He told his story to a monk who was one of his disciples. This is an example of the marvels wrought by Bishamonten. So the tale's been told, and so it's been handed down.

Notes to Story 44

1. Bridging a lacuna in the original; literally, "in ——— on Mount Hiei." Mount Hiei, overlooking the capital from the northeast, was the site of the Enryakuji, monastic center of the powerful Tendai school of Buddhism. A Buddhist temple comprises a number of separate buildings; at one time there were over three thousand on Mount Hiei's steep slopes, many of these residences of the masters and their disciples.

2. Bishamonten is enshrined at Kuramadera; I have supplied his name in this sentence for clarity. Bishamonten is one of the Four Deva Kings who protect the Dharma of the Buddha, and in early belief he appears as a warrior deity; but in Japan he was chiefly worshipped as one of the seven gods of prosperity.

Chapter Nineteen

8. HOW A FALCONER IN THE WESTERN PART OF THE CAPITAL RENOUNCED SECULAR LIFE BECAUSE OF A DREAM

AT A TIME NOW PAST, in the western part of the capital, there was a man whose profession was falconry. [His name is no longer known.] He had numerous sons, and he taught falconry to them too. He loved falconry so much that he indulged in it day and night; waking or sleeping, he could think of nothing else. At night he would set a hawk on his fist and sit with it, waiting for the day; in the daytime he would go out into the fields and hunt pheasants until dark. At home he had seven or eight hawks on perches side by side,[1] and he kept anywhere from ten to twenty leashed dogs. When it was time for the summer feedings, he slaughtered countless living creatures.[2] In winter, for days on end, he went out into the fields to take pheasants. In spring he used what are known as call birds, going into the fields at dawn and listening for the pheasants to respond to the artificial cry. So he passed his days until gradually he grew old.

Now, he caught a cold and feeling ill and out of sorts could not sleep at night. Just before dawn he dozed off and dreamed that he was in a large funerary shed in Sagano. It seemed to him that he had been living in that shed for many years along with his wife and children. Winter had been very cold, but spring had arrived and it was a beautiful day. He'd like to sun himself and pick some greens, he thought, and led his wife and children out of the shed. The warmth felt good to them, and they scattered, some to pick greens, some to play, each wandering far from the shed. Wife and children drifted off to their separate amusements.

From somewhere near the grove north of Uzumasa[3] came the sounds of many human voices and the ringing of numerous large and small bells. His chest constricted with terror, he went up to a high place to look. The men wore brocade caps and dappled hunting dress with bearskin chaps; at their waists they had curved swords in dappled boarskin pouches, and on their fists perched hawks like oni, to which high-pitched bells were fastened. The hawks flew up and were drawn back to the men's hands. Mounted on spirited horses, the men rode into Sagano and spread out into the fields. Before them came other men, who wore rush hats and blue hunting dress, with red leather sleeves on their arms and leather trousers, with wrappings around their shins and fur boots on their feet.[4] They pounded the grass with staves. The dogs were like lions: the large bells hung on them clanged so that the skies resounded; and they were swift as peregrines. At the sight his eyes grew dim and his mind grew numb. "I'll call my wife and children together at once, and we'll hide," he thought, but he saw that they were all off playing in different places: impossible to summon them. Hardly knowing one direction from another, he hid in a deep thicket. He saw that his cherished eldest son, Tarō, was also hiding in a thicket.

The dog handlers and falconers had spread out through the field. The dog handlers were flailing the thickets with staves and making the dogs sniff out scents. How terrible it was! And what was he to do? One handler came to the thicket where his eldest son was hiding and beat all the thick-growing pampas grass flat. Bell clanging, the dog came nearer, nose to the ground. "It's all up with him," he thought; and just then his son could bear it no longer and flew into the air. At this moment the dog barked loudly, and a falconer, who had withdrawn a short distance, let loose his hawk for the attack. Tarō flew up high, and the hawk went at his wings from below. Exhausted, Tarō slipped downward, and the hawk flew at him from below, gripped his head and belly, and sent him tumbling to the ground. The dog handler ran up, pulled the hawk loose, picked up Tarō and wrung his neck. The father heard Tarō's pitiful cries and felt that he himself could not go on living: it was as though a sword had cut his guts asunder.

"How is my second son faring?" he wondered. A dog also went sniffing toward the thicket where Jirō was hiding. As he watched, horrified, the dog rushed in and took Jirō in its mouth. Jirō spread his wings in fright, but the handler ran upon him and wrung his neck.

"And what about my third son?" As he looked toward the thicket where Saburō was hiding, a dog approached it sniffing. Saburō could not bear it and started up, whereupon the dog handler hit him on the head with the staff, clubbing him to the ground. "My children all are dead. Oh, if only my wife can be spared!" he thought in his grief—but even before the handler's approach his wife flew up and fled toward the mountains to the north. A falconer saw her, loosed his hawk, and galloped upon her. The wife flew as fast as she could and dropped down into a thicket at the base of a pine tree far away. A dog went straight to her and took her in its mouth.

The hawk perched in a tree and the falconer brought it back to his fist. The grass in the thicket in which he was hiding was high and the thorns were thick, so that he was well concealed; but not one but five or six dogs came toward him, bells ringing. He could bear it no longer and flew toward the mountains to the north, whereupon numbers of hawks came after him, some flying low, some flying high. Below, many dogs chased him, bells ringing. The falconers galloped their horses, while the dog handlers beat the thickets. Flying for his life, he barely managed to drop down into a deep clump of grass. The hawks perched in a high tree, ringing their bells to show the dogs where he was. The dogs followed the hawks' signal and came to sniff out the place he had fled to. There was no escape at all. The handlers urged the dogs on; their voices sounded like thunder. Alas! what could he do? He lay with his head hidden in the mire under the thicket and his butt sticking up. The dogs came nearer, bells ringing. "It's all over with me," he thought—and then he awoke.

He was bathed in perspiration. "It was a dream!" he thought. "What I dreamed of was the hawking I've been doing for years. I've killed a lot of pheasants in those years. Tonight I felt what the pheasants feel." He suddenly realized the boundlessness of his sins. Too impatient to await the dawn, he went to his hawk-house and sliced through the jesses of every one of his hawks on their perches and let them go free. He cut the leashes of his dogs and chased them away. He gathered up all of his gear for hawks and dogs and put it in the fire. Afterwards he spoke to his wife and children, tearfully telling them of his dream; and he went immediately to a holy mountain temple, cut off his topknot, and became a priest.

He became a holy man, devoted solely to his religious exercises. He chanted the invocation to Amida day and night, and when he died more than ten years later it was as a man who is revered. Truly his story commands our reverence. So the tale's been told, and so it's been handed down.

124 *Konjaku monogatari shū*

Notes to Story 8

1. A highly improbable number. Professor E. W. Jameson of the Zoology Department, University of California, Davis, has pointed out to me that hawks cannot usually be kept or flown together because they will fight. Falcons can, but they were infrequently used in Japan. But the whole tendency of this story is to exaggerate. I am extremely grateful to Prof. Jameson for elucidating this and other points in the story.

2. The hawks were then in molt, were not flown, and had to be given an especially rich diet.

3. To the west of the capital and south of Sagano. The bells attached to the tail feathers of hawks can be heard for half a mile or more.

4. These are precise descriptions of the traditional costumes of Japanese austringers and the dog handlers who assisted them.

24. ABOUT THE MONK WHOSE NAME WAS ENTERED ON A PETITION TO THE LORD OF MOUNT T'AI TO TAKE THE PLACE OF HIS MASTER

AT A TIME NOW PAST, there was a man [whose name is no longer known]. He was a monk [of what temple also is not known]. His eminence was such that he was honored both by the emperor and by private individuals. He contracted a grave illness and suffered painfully. His condition worsened as the days passed. In their distress his worthy, high-ranking disciples used every art they knew to pray for his recovery, but without the slightest success.

Now there was a Taoist doctor named Abe no Seimei,[1] the most eminent practitioner of his science, employed on that account both by the emperor and by private individuals. The disciples summoned this man in order to have him perform ceremonies to the Lord of Mount T'ai[2] and thereby cure their master's illness and save his life. Seimei came to them and said, "I have divined the course of this illness: it will be mortal. Even though I pray to the Lord of Mount T'ai I cannot save him. There is only one remedy: put forth one of your number who will die in place of the sick man. If you do, I will enter that monk's name on a petition to the god, proposing him as a substitute. Otherwise there is nothing I can do."

There was not one disciple who upon hearing this thought, "Let me sacrifice my own life for my master." Each wanted to save him, but without harm to himself. And, moreover, it occurred to the disciples that if he should die, they would inherit his chambers, his wealth, and his holy books. It was natural that no one felt in the least like substituting for him. They sat there side by side, staring into each other's faces, and nobody said a word.

For years there had been an under-disciple, a man of no consequence, who lived among them. The master scarcely deigned to notice him, and as he was poor, he inhabited a storage shed. When he heard the news he said, "My allotted years are already more than half gone. Who knows how much longer I may be going to live? And I'm poor: in the future I won't have the means to plant the roots of good karma. Since I must die in any event, let me do it now, in place of my master. Enter my name on the petition immediately." When they heard this, the other disciples thought, "What a noble mind!" And though none of them had been willing to sacrifice himself for the master, they were moved by his words, and many wept.

When Seimei heard this, he entered the monk's name on the petition of worship and performed the ceremonies with great care. And when the master heard of this, he said, "In all the years this monk has been here I never imagined that he was a man of such feeling," and he wept. As soon as the ceremonies were over, the master's illness subsided markedly: it appeared that the prayers were efficacious. It was thought, therefore, that the substitute would certainly die, and so a place was prepared for him to defile.[3] The monk disposed of his few possessions, gave what last instructions he had, and went to the place where he was to die. There he sat all alone, reciting the invocation to Amida. The others listened all night long, expecting him to die at any moment; but they heard nothing, and soon it was dawn.

The monk was supposed to die, but he was still alive. The master had already recovered. "No doubt the monk will die today," they were deciding as, early that morning, Seimei arrived. He said, "The master need fear no more; nor need the monk who offered himself as substitute have any fear. I have been able to save the lives of both." He departed, and master and disciples alike wept unrestrainedly for joy upon hearing his words.

Now think: the powers that rule over the world of the dead were moved to pity when the monk offered to substitute for his master, and they spared the lives of both. Everyone who heard of this praised and honored the monk. Thenceforth the master felt compassion for this monk and whenever the opportunity arose treated him as of more consequence than his high-ranking disciples; and truly he had reason to do so. Here indeed was a disciple with a rare heart. Both master and disciple lived to a ripe old age. So the tale's been told, and so it's been handed down.

Notes to Story 24

1. Seimei (911–1005) was a member of the lower nobility and the most eminent scion of a family of Taoist practitioners; other legends of his feats of divination and magic are translated in Mills, pp. 175–176, 339–341, 411–412.

2. The Lord of Mount T'ai (T'ai-shan Kung) was the Taoist counterpart to King Yama; in addition to presiding over hell, however, the god was also thought to have charge of the length of life of each individual.

3. In native Japanese belief death was defiling.

Chapter Twenty

35. HOW SHINKAI, A MONK OF MOUNT HIEI, SUFFERED RETRIBUTION IN THIS PRESENT LIFE FOR JEALOUSY

AT A TIME NOW PAST, in the East Pagoda of Mount Hiei,[1] there was a monk named Shinkai. On the Mountain he studied the Dharma, but since he was young and had no special talent, he could not obtain a place there. In those days there was a governor of Mino Province [whose name is no longer known];[2] the monk attached himself to this man and went out to the province as his follower. The governor's wife's old wet-nurse adopted him as a foster son, and because of this relationship the governor himself looked out for his interests as the occasion arose. The people of the province therefore called him the First Royal Priest[3] and showed him unbounded reverence.

Now an epidemic broke out in the province, and many took ill and died. Bewailing their misfortune, the people sent word to the governor, who was then in the capital. All strove together to prepare for a performance of the Hundred Lectures on the Sutra of the Benevolent Kings, to take place in front of a shrine called the Nangū.[4] Every effort was expended to make sure that this great Dharma assembly would be celebrated with utmost splendor and exactly as described in the sutra. Everyone in the province was relying on it, certain that it would produce the supernatural benefits so desperately needed. Everyone contributed. Rows of banners were hung, a thousand lamps were lit, and music was played.

A man named Kaikoku, a Royal Priest, was invited to be the principal lecturer. This Royal Priest was younger brother to the governor of Chikuzen, Minamoto Michinari Ason.[5] He was exceptionally learned and was a skillful and lively preacher; moreover, like his brother he was an accomplished poet and a good talker. All the fashionable laymen sought his friendship. He played and amused himself, a monk who was a celebrity. For years he served among the monks who recited the sutras at the

court of Emperor Go-Ichijō,[6] but when the Emperor died the
world changed and his fortunes with it, and he felt mournful
indeed. "I've grown old, and I've no prospects. It would be hard
even to get the office of acharya.[7] The lord who was my benefac-
tor is dead. Even if I should remain in society, what good would it
do me now?" And with this realization, all at once faith arose in
his heart, and he went to Mino, where he dwelled as a hermit in a
most holy mountain temple. "We should certainly make a point
of inviting a man of such eminence to be the principal lecturer.
How lucky that he is living in our province," the people thought,
and so they invited him.

Now, he had been a man of the highest rank and reputation on
Mount Hiei, and there were living on the Mountain a number of
his disciples, themselves men of no little distinction. "Let us first
sound him out," they said, and told him in private of the
intended invitation. The monk said, "I understand that the ceremony is to pray for the welfare of the province. I have made this
province my home and experienced its benefactions. Of course I
will serve! I will be there without fail."

The day arrived, and at length the ceremony began. The monk
left his mountain hermitage for temporary quarters, where he set
his robes to rights and waited. With a palanquin and parasols,
with music playing, all in good order came the welcoming procession. The lecturer took his censer and got into the palanquin; a
parasol was placed over it, and he was carried to his pulpit. The
other lecturers, too, a hundred men strong, mounted their
pulpits. A hundred Buddha images, a hundred bodhisattva images, a hundred arhat images, all beautifully painted, had been
hung up side by side. The vases held artificial flowers of every
variety, and the altar tables were filled with offerings in beautiful
colors.

Just as the principal lecturer was raising his eyes to the Buddha
image for the initial invocation, there appeared behind the pulpit
the First Royal Priest, accompanied by seven or eight ferocious-
looking monks wearing black-bordered stoles and tucked-up trousers[8] and brandishing pikeswords. The newcomer stopped some
twenty paces behind the pulpit, thumped his sides pugnaciously,
and holding up a fan for attention, said in fury, "This eminent
monk, this lecturer of yours, may be everyone's superior on
Mount Hiei, but in this province his lordship the governor has

appointed me to be the first of the monks. I don't know about other provinces — but in this province we don't worry about who's eminent and who's not: I'm the First Royal Priest in this province, and you should have invited me to be the merit-making lecturer. This gentleman is of the highest rank and I'm a mere nobody, but it's me you're supposed to ask, and to invite him while overlooking me — isn't that the height of insolence toward his lordship! I won't let him officiate today, whether the ceremony's completed or not. Well, that's just too bad! Come on, monks! Go to his reverence's seat and turn it over."

With that, the armed monks closed in to overturn the principal lecturer's pulpit. The lecturer leaped down from his seat; as he was short, he toppled head over heels. The monks who attended him took him in their arms and fled. Thereupon the First Priest jumped up in his place and in fury performed the lecturer's office.

The other lecturers were beside themselves; their tasks could not be performed, and the ceremony fell into utter confusion. The spectators who were not personally known to the First Priest feared getting involved and ran away behind his back, so that only a few people remained. When the rites were finished all the gifts that had been prepared for the principal lecturer were given to the First Priest. Those persons of the province who had stayed behind betrayed by the expressions on their faces that the ceremony had not been at all what they had had in mind.

Some months later, when the governor's term of office was over, the First Royal Priest followed him back to the capital. The governor died after only a few years, and the First Priest, left without a patron, was quite without means of support. Not only that, but he contracted a kind of leprosy in which the skin turns white. Even the old nurse who had vowed to be a parent to him thought him unclean and would not let him come near. With nowhere to go, he took refuge in a hut among the beggars at Kiyomizu and Sakamoto.[9] Even there, among the crippled and deformed, he was held in abomination; and after three months he died.

This is nothing less than the truth. Because this man obstructed a solemn Dharma assembly and, himself of low degree, was jealous of a monk of the highest rank and reputation, he suffered karmic retribution in this same life.

People who know of this will never let jealousy arise in their hearts. Heaven abominates jealousy. So the tale's been told, and so it's been handed down.

Notes to Story 35

1. See 17:44, note 1. It should be observed that both of the men in this story — the formerly worldly one as well as the ineptly worldly one — came originally from Mount Hiei.

2. Mino was in modern Gifu prefecture.

3. *Gubu*, or *naigubu*, one of the select group of monks appointed to participate in religious services within the imperial palace enclosure.

4. Ceremonies of lectures on the Sutra of the Benevolent Kings were performed at frequent intervals, particularly in the capital, for they were thought to be a potent means of pacifying the demons who might otherwise cause epidemics and natural disasters. Both the benefits to be derived from the ceremony and the manner in which it is to be carried out are described in the sutra itself (*Taishō shinshū daizōkyō* 245. 830a.1-b.2): the hundred lecturers, hundred pulpits, Buddha, bodhisattva, and arhat images, the lamps, flowers (a hundred varieties), music, and even the offerings to the officiants mentioned in the story are all stipulated in the sutra. When the number of lectures is part of the name of a ceremony (e.g., the Eight Lectures on the Lotus Sutra), the meaning is ordinarily that the lectures were given successively, over a period of days or even weeks. In this case, however, the Hundred Lectures were evidently to be given simultaneously, for they were to be completed within four hours, and in the same place. Traditional lecturing seems often to have consisted of a recitation of the text accompanied by glossing of words and phrases; what was important, in any event, was that the lectures be carried out, not that they convey information to the human listeners present. Performance of the Hundred Lectures lapsed at the end of the Heian period, although at least one attempt has been made during the present century to reconstruct and revive the rite.

The exact location of the Nangū shrine is not known. It was not unusual at this time for Buddhist ceremonies to be performed at Shintō shrines.

5. Michinari, d. 1036, achieved senior fourth rank lower grade; poems by him appear in the imperial anthology *Goshūishū*. Ason is a *kabane*, or hereditary clan title. Note the circularity of the storytelling here: first we are told that Kaikoku was invited; then we are told how he came to be invited; then we are told in detail the manner in which the invitation was proffered.

6. Reigned 1016–1036, d. 1036.

7. Acharya: *ajari,* from a Sanskrit word meaning teacher, was the title of certain imperially appointed officers within Tendai and Shingon temples.

8. A stole worn over the left shoulder and under the right arm was one of the prescribed garments of every monk, but a stole of this description was supposed to be worn only by holders of high monastic office. Trouser hems were tucked up with drawstrings in readiness for violent physical exertion.

9. There are other references in *Konjaku* to Kiyomizu and Sakamoto as areas where beggars and lepers of the capital congregated.

Secular Tales of Japan

Chapter Twenty-one is lacking. Chapter Twenty-two, consisting in its present state of only eight tales, tells of the founding and rise of the Fujiwara family and the fortunes of its branches; and a concern with family continuity and the apportioning of power is present even when—as in the tale of Tokihira—the narrative seems to be at its most purely entertaining. Chapter Twenty-three was originally intended to consist of twenty-six tales but lacks the first twelve. Men of arms appear in this chapter, as well as in Chapter Twenty-five; one difference is that in the former chapter it is the mysteriousness of the feat he is recounting that most intrigues the storyteller, while in the latter it is likely to be the dedication of the warrior to his craft that is emphasized. The same intense self-dedication characterizes many of the artists and craftsmen whose stories appear in Chapter Twenty-four. Chapter Twenty-six contains a variety of stories; what they have in common is that each ends with a comment by the compiler that whatever has taken place must be the result of karma from the protagonists' previous lives. The tale that is translated here is of interest as an example of one kind of local legend. Chapter Twenty-seven brings together stories about supernatural creatures: oni and foxes and others about whose precise nature the compiler can only speculate. Chapter Twenty-eight, devoted to humor, is a popular one with modern Japanese readers, as is Chapter Twenty-nine, devoted principally to crimes of violence and their perpetrators. Chapter Thirty, described in the original as a miscellany, consists of love stories told in the traditional form of the poem-tale—a tale that climaxes with the composition or exchange of poems. Chapter Thirty-one is a true miscellany of strange tales and legends of high antiquity, and its story of the fabled oak of Ōmi Province closes the book.

Chapter Twenty-Two

8. HOW GREAT MINISTER TOKIHIRA
GOT MAJOR COUNSELOR KUNITSUNE'S WIFE

AT A TIME NOW PAST, there was a man known as the Hon'in Great Minister of the Left. His personal name was Tokihira; he was a son of the Civil Dictator Lord Shōsen, and he lived in a place called Hon'in. He was only thirty and as handsome as can be. The Engi emperor, you may be sure, thought the very world of this minister.[1]

Now, as is well known, this Emperor exercised firm rule; nevertheless, this Great Minister entered the palace grounds wearing clothes forbidden by the sumptuary laws. From his private window in the palace His Majesty saw him approach in magnificent attire and became wrathful. He immediately summoned a secretary and commanded: "Recently I have issued strict injunctions against luxury. First among my ministers though he is, he has no right to enter the palace in such splendid clothes. How dare he! Order him to leave at once."

The secretary was most alarmed at the Emperor's words; trembling from head to foot, he reported them to the Great Minister, who with signs of the most extreme respect hastened to withdraw. Bodyguards and official attendants had accompanied him to the Presence, but by command no voices were raised to clear the way for his return procession. His outriders did not know the circumstances and thought this very odd. For a month thereafter he kept the gates of his mansion shut and never so much as stepped outside his chamber. When people came to call he refused to see them. "It is because of the severity of His Majesty's censure," they were told. At the end of this period he was readmitted to the Imperial Presence. In actuality he had concocted the entire incident with the Emperor beforehand, as a warning to others.

This Minister's one failing, it seems, was his penchant for womanizing. He had an uncle, Major Counselor Kunitsune, whose wife was the daughter of [a member of][2] the Ariwara family. The Major Counselor was eighty years old, his wife no more than twenty. She was beautiful and flirtatious, and she was not at all pleased at finding herself married to an elderly husband. Amorist that he was, the Minister had got wind of his uncle's lady's charms. He burned with curiosity to see her, but for a long time he could think of no means of effecting a meeting.

Among his contemporaries was a man named Taira no Sadabumi, a Captain of the Guards and a man of good birth, the grandson of a prince; his nickname was Heichū. He was the most assiduous amorist of his day, and there were few indeed among other people's wives and daughters and among the ladies-in-waiting in the palace whom he had not visited behind their screens.[3]

This Heichū was a constant caller at the Great Minister's house. Might *he* perhaps have viewed his uncle the Counselor's wife? the Minister wondered. One moonlit winter evening Heichū came for a visit. The Minister chatted with him about one thing and another as the night deepened. All sorts of amusing topics cropped up, and in the course of the conversation the Minister said to Heichū, "If you think I speak honestly with you, be open with me. Tell me: who among the women of today is the fairest?"

"What an awkward question! But you say 'be open with me,' so I will. There is no one in all the world who can compare with the wife of your uncle the Major Counselor."

"But how did you manage to see her?" said the Minister.

"I knew someone in service there. 'She's miserable as can be at being married to an old man,' I was told; so I thought up an excuse to have my acquaintance speak to her on my behalf. She rather fancied me, I was told. On the spur of the moment I sneaked in to meet her. It wasn't what you'd call an *intimate* meeting."

"You wretch, you bungled it!" cried the Minister, laughing.

His determination by some means or other to meet this woman grew ever stronger.

Since the Counselor was his uncle, the Minister thenceforward made a point of consulting him respectfully whenever the occasion arose. The Counselor was touched and grateful. He had no idea that the Minister proposed to steal his wife, and the Minister was secretly amused.

The New Year came around. Though he had never done anything of the sort before, the Minister sent word to the Counselor that he would come for a visit on one of the first three days of the month.[4] At this announcement the Counselor refurbished his house and made elaborate arrangements to receive the guest. On the third day the Minister arrived, accompanied by a modest retinue of high-ranking noblemen. The Counselor could scarcely contain his delight. Here was justification for all his preparations.

It was late in the afternoon when the Minister arrived, and the sun went down while round upon round of saké was consumed. There was singing, and the party had a fine time. The Great Minister of the Left was among those who sang, and he cut an incomparably splendid figure. Everyone's eyes were fixed on him admiringly. The Counselor's lady observed him closely, for the blinds she sat behind were next to his seat, and everything about him—his face, his beautiful singing voice, the sumptuous scent of his clothing (just to start with)—was finer than anything she had ever seen before. How cruel was her own fate! What sort of woman might be the wife of such a man? she wondered. And to think that she for her part had to put up with a husband who stank of old age! The more she looked at the Minister, the greater became her agitation and her misery. As he sang the Minister continually cast sidelong glances toward the blinds. Her shame was indescribable; even hidden by the blinds she could scarcely endure it. What must he be thinking of her, she wondered, humiliated, as the Minister gazed toward her, all smiles.

Little by little it got to be very late. The whole party was well gone in drink. All present loosened their sashes and overrobes and danced with unrestrained merriment.

Soon it was time for the guests to depart. The Counselor said to the Minister, "You seem rather drunk. Please have your carriage brought all the way up to the house, so you can get in it from here."[5]

"That would be much too rude," said the Minister. "Why, I could never do such a thing! I'm very drunk, but I'll just stay here until I've sobered up a bit, then I'll be on my way."

"Yes, that would be by far the best," the other noblemen said; nevertheless, the carriage was brought up in front of the center staircase. The Counselor brought out the farewell presents: two magnificent horses, a thirteen-string koto, and other things.

The Minister said to the Counselor, "Excuse my bluntness, it's because I'm drunk. I came to do the family honors. Are you truly glad to see me? Then give me some parting gift that will specially please me."

In the depths of his own drunkenness the Counselor was overcome with joy at the thought that the first minister of the land had paid him a visit—for uncle though he was, he himself was only a Counselor. He had noted uneasily the sidelong glances which the Minister had continually directed toward the blinds; he was annoyed, and it occurred to him to show his nephew what sort of wife he had. Crazed with drink, he said, "Look what I have—a beautiful young wife. You're a fine minister to be sure, but you can have no one like her. Just fancy her living with an old codger! I'll let her be your parting gift," and he pushed the screens aside, thrust his hand behind the blinds, and pulled the lady out by her sleeve. "Here she is," he said.

"I'm delighted," said the Minister. "My visit has been well rewarded." He grasped the lady's sleeve and drew her to his seat. The Counselor got up and turned to go, signing with a gesture of his hand that the other gentlemen might leave now; the Minister would not be going for quite some time. The companions winked at each other; some went away, while others hid and waited to see what would happen.

"I'm drunk all right," said the Minister. "Well then, bring the carriage up. It can't be helped."

The carriage was already in the courtyard; now a great many men approached and pulled it the rest of the way up to the house. The Counselor came forward and personally raised the carriage blinds. The Minister picked up the Counselor's lady in his arms and put her inside, then without further ado got in himself. Helpless, the Counselor said, "Now, now, granny, don't forget me."

The Minister had the carriage driven out the gate and returned home.

The Counselor went indoors, loosened his clothing, and lay down; so drunk he couldn't see straight, and feeling ill, he fell asleep, oblivious to everything. At dawn he woke up sober. He recalled the events of the night before as in a dream. It was a dream, wasn't it? "Where is her ladyship?" he asked the waiting-woman beside him. When the waiting-woman told him what had taken place he was flabbergasted. "I was overjoyed, true—but I went mad! Drunk or not, has anyone ever seen the like?" he groaned; and this self-reproach was even more unbearable than the loss of his lady. Since there was no way of getting her back, he tried to pretend to himself that it was for the sake of the lady's happiness. But that she had let it be seen that she thought him too old! Chagrined, jealous, sad, loving, he tried to make others think that was what he himself had wanted, but in his heart he remained hopelessly in love. [The manuscript breaks off here.]

Notes to Story 8

1. Fujiwara Tokihira, 868–906; Shōsen was the posthumous name of Fujiwara Motokiyo, 836–891; the Engi emperor (i.e., the emperor who was on the throne during the Engi era) was Daigo, r. 897–930, whose reign was looked upon in later times as a model of imperial rule. The Civil Dictator *(kanpaku)* was de facto head of the government and chief of the Fujiwara clan. At times when the office of Prime Minister *(dajō daijin)* was vacant, the Great Minister of the Left *(sadaijin)* was the highest-ranking officer in the government.

2. There is a lacuna in the original where the lady's father's given name should appear. The consensus among commentators is that he was Ariwara Muneyana.

3. Taira Sadabumi (d. 923) was celebrated both as a poet and as a lover. He is the subject of a work called *Heichū monogatari,* most likely compiled between 959 and 965, and also of four episodes in the poem-tale collection *Yamato monogatari,* compiled 951 or 952; these latter have been translated by Mildred Tahara, "Heichū, as Seen in Yamato Monogatari," *Monumenta Nipponica,* vol. 26 (1971), pp. 17–48. The 124th tale in *Yamato monogatari* describes Sadabumi's wooing of the lady in the present story. His suit there was more successful. Perhaps because of his passivity, as compared with another romantic hero and poet, Ariwara Narihira, Sadabumi became increasingly a figure of fun (see Yoneda Chizuko, "Heichū setsuwa to warai keifu," in Kanda Hideo and Kunisaki Fumimaro, eds., *Nihon no setsuwa,* vol. 1 [1947], pp. 407–427). By the time of *Konjaku* he was well established in the character of a failure in love. There is a comical reference to him in the Suetsumuhana ("Safflower") chapter of the *Tale of Genji.*

4. As Major Counselor *(dainagon),* Kunitsune was Tokihira's inferior in rank. It was exceptional at this time for a superior to visit an inferior; such a visit was a mark of considerable esteem.

5. Carriages ordinarily remained at one of the outer gates of the courtyard and were only brought up to the main house when someone was ill or incapacitated. Here the Counselor is about to win the politeness contest.

Chapter Twenty-Three

14. HOW TAIRA NO MUNETSUNE, LIEUTENANT OF THE LEFT DIVISION OF THE OUTER PALACE GUARDS, ESCORTED HIGH PRIEST MYŌSON

AT A TIME NOW PAST, when the Lord of Uji was in his glory,[1] he had in attendance on him one night High Priest Myōson of Miidera.[2] No lamps were lit, and after a short time his lordship suddenly decided to send the High Priest on an errand—what exactly, one doesn't know, but he was to go and return again the same night. A horse was saddled for him in his lordship's stables, one that would not shy or bolt. "Who will accompany him?" inquired his lordship when the horse had been led out. Taira no Munetsune, lieutenant of the Left Division of the Outer Palace Guards, announced himself. "Excellent," said his lordship. "The Assistant High Priest must go to Miidera tonight," his lordship announced (at that time the High Priest was Assistant High Priest), "and return immediately. He is to be back before the night is over. You are responsible for his safety." Munetsune listened to the order. In the barracks he always kept bow and quiver in readiness, and he had a pair of straw sandals hidden under a mat. He retained only a single attendant, a base-born servant, so that people who saw him thought, "What a stingy mean fellow he is!" Upon receiving the order, then, he tucked up his trouser hems, groped about until he had found his sandals, put them on, strapped the quiver to his back, and went over to where the horse had been led out for Myōson. He stationed himself beside it.

"Who are you?" asked the priest.

"Munetsune," he replied.

"We shall be going to Miidera," said the priest. "Why have you prepared yourself to go on foot? Have you no mount?"

"Even if I'm on foot I won't fall behind, never fear. Only make haste yourself," he said.

The priest thought this all very strange. Torchbearers were

sent out ahead. The two had traveled seven or eight hundred yards when two men dressed in black and armed with bows and arrows came toward them on foot. The priest was frightened, but the two men fell to their knees the moment they saw Munetsune. "Your horse, sir," they said. They had led horses out; since it was night, the color of the horses could not be made out. The men were carrying riding shoes for Munetsune. Munetsune put these on over his straw sandals and mounted a horse. Now that there were two men, mounted and armed, accompanying, the priest felt easy in mind. They proceeded another two hundred yards, and from the side of the road there appeared two more bowmen dressed in black, who prostrated themselves just as before. Munetsune said not a word on either occasion. They mounted the horses they had led out and joined the escort. No doubt these too were Munetsune's retainers — but what a queer way he goes about his business! the priest thought. And then two hundred yards farther on two more men appeared and joined them in the same way. Again Munetsune said not a word; and the new companions said not a word. Whenever the party had gone a hundred yards and yet another hundred, two more men were added to their number, so that by the time they reached the banks of the Kamo River there were more than thirty. What a queer way he goes about his business! the High Priest thought, and thus they arrived at Miidera.

He attended to the affair he had been charged with and started back before midnight. Before him, behind him, surrounding him, rode Munetsune's retainers. He felt very much at ease. The escort rode in a body as far as the Kamo River banks. After they reentered the capital, though Munetsune said not a word, the men dropped off two at a time at the places from which they had emerged, so that when his lordship's mansion was only a hundred yards away there remained only the two companions who had appeared first. At the spot at which he had mounted his horse, Munetsune dismounted and took off the shoes he had put on, so that now he was dressed as he had been when he left. He walked away as the two men vanished into the shadows with his shoes and the horse. Accompanied only by his servant and wearing straw sandals, he went on foot through the gate of his lordship's mansion.

The High Priest was astounded at what he had witnessed. He thought it utterly uncanny, how horses and men performed as though rehearsed and instructed beforehand. "I'll tell his lordship about it at the first opportunity," he thought as he went into his presence. The lord had waited up for him. The priest reported on the discharge of his own commission; then he said, "Munetsune certainly goes about his business queerly," and related everything that had happened. "What splendid followers he has!" he added.

His lordship listened. "Surely he'll question me further," the priest thought, but—whatever the lord was thinking—he did not, and the priest's expectation was frustrated.

This Munetsune was the son of a warrior named Taira no Muneyori.[3] He was fierce and bold, and he shot especially large arrows unlike those used by ordinary marksmen. For that reason people called him the Large Arrow Lieutenant. So the tale's been told, and so it's been handed down.

Notes to Story 14

1. The Lord of Uji was Fujiwara Yorimichi (992–1074), son of the all-powerful Michinaga; the incident narrated here seems to have taken place some time between 1021 and 1028.

2. Myōson (the name is also read Myōzon): 971–1063. Miidera is another name for the Tendai temple Onjōji, in modern Ōtsu, east of Kyoto. Myōson was in attendance on the lord in order to perform the rituals that warded away illness.

3. Muneyori (d. 1011) was a popular subject of anecdote. The story immediately preceding the present one deals with a private war that he fought with another provincial warrior. He reappears in *Konjaku* 31:24 as the leader of a hired army in a brawl between two monasteries.

Chapter Twenty-Four

2. HOW PRINCE KAYA MADE A DOLL AND SET IT UP IN THE RICEFIELDS

AT A TIME NOW PAST, there was a man named Prince Kaya who was a son of Emperor [Kanmu].[1] He was an extraordinarily skilled craftsman. There was a temple called Kyōgokuji, which the prince had established.[2] It derived its income from the ricefields before it. These lay along the banks of the Kamo River.

One year there was a drought throughout the kingdom, and everywhere there were loud complaints of ricefields seared and dead. The temple's fields were in especial danger, for it was water from the Kamo River that irrigated them, and that river had dried up entirely. Soon the ricefields would become as barren ground, and the seedlings would redden and die.

Prince Kaya, however, contrived as follows. He made a doll in the shape of a boy about feet tall, holding a jug upraised in both hands. It was devised so that when it was filled with water the water would instantly pour down over the boy's face. Those who saw it brought ladles full of water so that they could fill the jug and watch the boy's face get wet. It was a great curiosity; the news spread, and soon all the capital was there, pouring water and loudly enjoying the fun. And all the while, naturally, the water was collecting in the fields. When the fields were fully inundated, the Prince took the doll and hid it. And when the water dried up, he took the doll out and set it up again. Just as before, people gathered to pour water, and the fields were inundated. In this manner the fields were kept safe from harm.

This was a splendid device; and the Prince was praised to the skies for his ingenuity and skill. So the tale's been told, and so it's been handed down.[3]

Notes to Story 2

1. Lacuna in the original. Kanmu r. 781–806; Prince Kaya (794–871) was his seventh son.

2. The temple was situated on a large plot of ground near the eastern boundary of Kyoto, at Third Avenue.

3. There are numerous precedents for the theme of this story in Chinese literature, and this story may well be of Chinese inspiration. "There was Yang Wu-lien, afterwards a general, who made a figure of a monk which stretched out its hand for contributions, saying 'Alms! Alms!' and depositing the contributions in its satchel when they reached a certain weight" (Joseph Needham, *Science and Civilisation in China* [Cambridge, England], vol. 4, part 2 [1964], p. 163).

23. HOW MINAMOTO NO HIROMASA ASON WENT TO THE BLIND MAN'S HOUSE AT ŌSAKA

AT A TIME NOW PAST, there was a man named Minamoto no Hiromasa Ason. He was son of a prince who was Minister of War and himself a son of the Engi emperor. He was a master of all the arts and sciences, but among them, especially, the Way of musical instruments. His skill at the lute was amazing, the beauty of his flute-playing indescribable. He was a courtier of middle rank during the reign of Emperor Murakami.[1]

At this time there was a blind man who had built himself a hut to live in at the barrier of Ōsaka. His name was Semimaro.[2] He had once been no more than a menial attendant in the household of Prince Atsumi, the Minister of Ceremonial. That Prince was a son of the cloistered emperor Uda and had mastered the Way of musical instruments. Year after year Semimaro had constantly heard him play the lute, until he himself grew amazingly skillful at it.

Now Hiromasa was passionately fond of the Way of music and passionately eager to learn everything related to it, so that when he heard that the blind man who lived at the Ōsaka barrier was a proficient musician he decided that he simply had to hear him. But the blind man's house was so singular that, instead of going there, he sent a servant to speak to Semimaro in private. "Why do you live in such a strange place? Suppose you were to come to the capital to live?"

The blind man heard this and made no reply, only speaking this verse:

> *In this world*
> *No matter how*
> *We pass our days —*
> *Neither palace nor hovel*
> *Is our final dwelling.*

The messenger returned and recounted this. Hiromasa was impressed with the blind man's gentility. He thought to himself, "It is because of my devotion to this Way that I am profoundly convinced that I must meet him. Furthermore, it's hard to tell how much longer the blind man may live; nor do I know how long my own life will last. There are two tunes for lute called 'Flowing Spring' and 'Woodpecker' that are likely to become extinct with this generation. They say that only this blind man knows them. Somehow or other I'll contrive to hear him play them."

With this in view, he journeyed one night to the barrier at Ōsaka. Semimaro, however, never once played those tunes. And so, thereafter, night after night for three long years, he journeyed to the hut at Ōsaka. He hid himself and waited, listening: would he play tonight? Would he play tonight? But the blind man never played at all.

In the third year, on the night of the fifteenth day of the eighth month, a fine mist lay over the face of the moon and a gentle breeze was blowing. "What a charming evening it is!" thought Hiromasa. "Surely this night the blind man of Ōsaka will play 'Flowing Spring' and 'Woodpecker.' " He went to Ōsaka, and as he waited, listening, the blind man plucked the strings, with the expression of one who is deeply moved. Hiromasa listened with mounting joy as the blind man, to cheer his loneliness, chanted this poem:

> *The stormwinds*
> *At Ōsaka barrier*
> *Are wild;*
> *Yet here I spend my days*
> *Stubbornly, blind.*

As he made the lute sound, Hiromasa felt the tears stream down his face.

The blind man was speaking to himself. "Ah, it is a charming night. I wonder if somewhere there is someone besides myself who appreciates it. If only a visitor would come who understood my art. We should talk together."[3]

Hiromasa heard this and spoke up: "A man named Hiromasa who lives in the capital has in fact come here." "By whom have I the honor to be addressed?" said the blind man. Hiromasa told his name and origin. "Because I am devoted to this Way, for the past three years I have come to your hut. Tonight, to my great good fortune, I have met you." The blind man heard this and rejoiced. Thereupon, Hiromasa, in the midst of his own rejoicing, entered the hut. Together they talked. Hiromasa said, "I should like to hear 'Flowing Spring' and 'Woodpecker.'" "His late lordship played them this way," said the blind man, and transmitted the knowledge of the pieces in question to Hiromasa. Hiromasa had not brought his lute with him, and so he learned them orally. Over and over again he gave thanks. At dawn he returned home.

Now think: this is the sort of devotion that should be shown toward each of the many Ways. In this Latter Age, men who have achieved mastery in the various Ways are few. Truly this is a deplorable state of affairs.[4]

Though Semimaro was a base-born fellow, through hearing the Prince play the lute year after year he acquired consummate skill. It was because he had gone blind that he was living at Ōsaka. The tradition of blind lute-players begins from that time. So the tale's been told, and so it's been handed down.

Notes to Story 23

1. The Engi emperor was Emperor Daigo, reigned 897–930. Emperor Murakami reigned 946–967. There is a lacuna in the final sentence of this paragraph which I have glossed over: Hiromasa (919–980) is described in the text as a *tenjōbito,* one of the courtiers, of fourth, fifth, and in some cases sixth rank, who were allowed to enter the imperial presence, and it has been suggested that the compiler left the space in order to fill in later his precise rank at this time. Hiromasa rose to the third rank before he died.

2. Ōsaka, not to be confused with the modern city of the same name, was a mountain pass a few miles east of modern Kyoto which was the site, during various eras, of a military checkpoint. Nothing is known of the historical Semimaro, or Semimaru. There is a book-length study of his legend and its evolution up to the present day, by Susan Matisoff, *The Legend of Semimaru: Blind Musician of Japan* (New York: Columbia University Press, 1978). Emperor Uda (below) reigned 887–897.

3. One of the pleasures of art. In a story about another sort of art (24:27), on this same night of the year, renowned for its beautiful moonlight, a group of old friends pay a sentimental visit to the deserted mansion of the late scholar of Chinese literature Ōe Asatsuna. As they are chanting Chinese poems, out of the shadows glides an aged crone. "You have misinterpreted that line," she says. "My late master used to recite it altogether differently." Like Semimaro, she had once been a menial servant—the great man's laundress! Years of overhearing his art had given her an expert knowledge denied the ordinary aspirant. The friends talk with her the night through and leave only after presenting parting gifts.

4. Anecdotes of this nature suggest some of the parallels between art and religion in Japanese tradition. Both art and religion demand total devotion. To acquire a secret tradition or become the disciple of a great man, the aspirant must demonstrate almost superhuman persistence; yet, a great master's influence is such that it may transform those who have come into contact with him simply through living in his household. The word which I have translated Way, capitalizing it, is the same as that for religious path (see, e.g., 1:8). And the Latter Age was the time of decline not only of the Buddha's Dharma but of the arts as well. It might be added that mastery of the arts can confer supernatural powers that resemble, though in lesser degree, those enjoyed by the religious adept; the perspicacity of Hiromasa in the story that follows, and his ability to talk an oni into submission, might be seen as an example.

24. HOW THE LUTE GENJŌ WAS SNATCHED BY AN ONI

AT A TIME NOW PAST, during the reign of Emperor Murakami, the lute Genjō suddenly disappeared. It was an imperial treasure, handed down through reign upon reign. The Emperor lamented bitterly the fact that so venerable an heirloom had been lost while he was on the throne. Perhaps it had been stolen—but if that were the case it would not have stayed out of sight for so long. It was feared that some person with a grudge against the Emperor had taken it and destroyed it.

Now, among the courtiers of middle rank there was a man named Minamoto no Hiromasa. He knew all there was to know of the Way of musical instruments. While he was brooding mournfully over Genjō's disappearance, he happened to be in the Seiryōden¹ at night after the noises of human activity were stilled, and he heard, from somewhere to the south, the sound of Genjō's strings. In his astonishment he wondered if he could have misheard. He listened carefully: it was none other than Genjō. There could be no mistake, and his wonder increased all the more. He told no one, but dressed informally as he was, he slipped on his shoes and went out past the palace guards' headquarters with only a page boy to attend him. He went southward; the sound seemed to be coming from somewhere ahead of him. It must be very near, he kept thinking — and soon he had come to Shujaku gate. It seemed to be yet farther ahead — and so he walked southward down Shujaku Avenue. He thought that whoever stole Genjō must be playing it in secret in a [certain] viewing pavilion. He hurried to the pavilion and listened: it sounded quite close by, and farther south. And thus he walked on toward the south until he was at Rashō gate.²

He stood under the gate and heard Genjō sounding from the upper story. "That's no human being playing the instrument," he thought in amazement. "It can only be an oni or some such being." The playing stopped and then resumed after a little while. "You there playing," said Hiromasa. "Who are you? Genjō was lost the other day; the Emperor's been searching everywhere. Tonight in the Seiryōden I heard it sound to the south, and so I've come after it."

At that moment the playing stopped and something came down from the ceiling. Hiromasa drew back in fear and saw that Genjō had been lowered at the end of a cord. Terrified though he was, he took the lute and carried it back to the palace, where he presented it to the Emperor with an account of what had happened. The Emperor was deeply moved. "So it was an oni that took it!" he exclaimed. All who heard of this praised Hiromasa.

The lute Genjō exists even today. It is in the palace, an imperial treasure handed down through reign upon reign. It is just like a

The oni lowers the lute Genjō
from the second story of Rashō gate.

living being. If it is played clumsily or incompletely, it becomes angry and won't resound. Also, if there is dust on it that isn't wiped away, it becomes angry and won't resound. You can tell its mood just by looking at it. Once there was a fire in the palace, and though no one carried it, it went out under its own power and was found in the courtyard.

An uncanny tale, isn't it! So the tale's been told, and so it's been handed down.

Notes to Story 24

1. The Seiryōden was the principal ceremonial hall in the imperial palace compound.

2. The palace compound was at the north end of the city. The Shujaku (or Suzaku) gate was at the south end of the compound and gave onto Shujaku Avenue. Rashō (or Rajō) gate was at the south end of the city. The latter gate is described in historical sources as splendidly ornamented, but it fell into disrepair at an early time, and its upper story — it was two-storied — was thought to be the abode of supernatural beings, and worse. We shall meet it again, in 29:18.

Chapter Twenty-Five

11. HOW FUJIWARA NO CHIKATAKA'S SON WAS TAKEN HOSTAGE BY A ROBBER AND FREED THROUGH YORINOBU'S PERSUASION

AT A TIME NOW PAST, when Minamoto no Yorinobu Ason, Governor of Kōchi, was Governor of Kōzuke[1] and residing in that province, there was in his retinue a man named Fujiwara no Chikataka, Lieutenant of the Middle Palace Guards, who was the son of Yorinobu's old nurse. Chikataka too was everything that a warrior should be. During the time that he was in Kōzuke with Yorinobu, he caught a thief and placed him under guard in his own house. Somehow or other the man managed to slip his shackles and get away. Chikataka's son, a pretty child of no more than five or six years, was running about. Perhaps because the thief saw no means of completing his escape, he seized the child as a hostage and took him into a storage shed.[2] There he forced him down between his knees. He drew a knife and sat there with the tip pressed to the child's belly.

Someone ran to the government office where Chikataka was. "A thief has taken the young master hostage," was the report. Chikataka hurried back in alarm. He saw it: it was true. The thief was sitting in the shed with a knife at the little boy's belly. The father grew faint at the sight. But what was he to do? It occurred to him that he might just go up and snatch the boy away—but there in full view was the knife, large and glittering, pressed to his boy's belly.

"Keep away! One step closer and I'll run him through," the thief said. "He'll kill him, just as he says," thought Chikataka. "I could hack the scoundrel to bits—but what good would it do?" To his followers he said, "Keep your wits about you. Don't get near. Surround him, but from a distance." And he ran to Yorinobu's office to inform him.

It was not far to go. The Governor was astonished to see Chikataka rush in, in evident consternation. "Is something the matter?" he asked. "My little boy, my only son, has been taken hostage by a robber," Chikataka said in tears.

The Governor laughed. "Not that you haven't cause," he said, "but what are you doing here weeping? You should want to put up a fight, even if it were with a god or a demon. You're weeping like a child! Isn't that ridiculous. You should think, 'Let him be killed if need be. He's only one little boy.' If that's how you can feel, you will fulfill your duty as a warrior. If you worry about your own safety, if you worry about your wife and child, you'll be beaten at every turn. Fearlessness means to have no thought for yourself or your family. All the same, though, I'll go have a look." And carrying only his long sword for a weapon, the Governor went to Chikataka's house.

The Governor stood at the entrance to the shed and peered inside. The thief saw that it was the Governor who was there, and instead of flaring up, as he had when he spoke to Chikataka, he lowered his eyes, gripping his knife all the harder to show that he was ready to run the boy through at the first attempt to come near. All the while the child was howling. The Governor addressed the thief: "You've taken this boy hostage. Was it in the hope of saving your life? Or did you simply want to kill him? Which is it? Speak up, scoundrel."

In a pitiful, thin voice the thief replied: "How could I think of killing a child, sir! It's only that I don't want to die. I wanted to stay alive, and I thought that taking a hostage might give me a chance."

"Then throw that knife away," said the Governor. "It is I who command you, I, Yorinobu. I don't intend to look on while you kill a child. I mean what I say, you know that: my reputation gets around. Just throw it away, thief!"

The thief considered a while. "Thank you, sir, I will. I wouldn't dare disobey you. I'll throw my knife away," and he flung it far away, jerked the boy to his feet, and released him. Once on his feet, the boy scampered off as fast as he could go.

The Governor withdrew a short distance and summoned his retainers. "Get that man over here," he said. The retainers took the thief by the collar and dragged him into the courtyard in front of the house. Chikataka wanted to cut him down with his sword, but the Governor said, "This fellow let his hostage go— now that's a fine thing to have done! He became a thief because he was poor; and he took a hostage in order to save his life. There's no need to hate him. After all, he did as I told him: that shows there's some sense in the scoundrel. Let him go at once." Turning to the thief, he said, "What do you need? Tell me," but the thief only wept speechlessly.

"Give him a few provisions," the Governor said. "He's done other bad deeds, and he's likely to end up killing someone. Look among the draft horses in the stable for one that's strong. Put a cheap saddle on it and bring it here." He sent men to fetch them. He also sent for a crude bow and quiver. When all had been brought out, he had the robber put the quiver on his back and mount the horse in the front courtyard. The men put ten days' worth of dried rice in a bag, wrapped it in a coarse sack, and fastened it to his waist.

"Now then, ride right out of here and begone!" Obedient to the Governor's command, the thief galloped away and was lost from sight.

It must have been the dread he felt at a single word from Yorinobu that made the thief release his hostage. Now think: never was there a more fearsome warrior than Yorinobu.

When the boy who had been taken hostage grew up, he abandoned secular life on Mount Mitake[3] and ultimately attained the office of acharya. His religious name was Myōshū. So the tale's been told, and so it's been handed down.

Notes to Story 11

1. This celebrated warrior (968–1048) is recorded as having been Governor of Kōzuke (modern Gunma prefecture) in 999. He came to be called Governor of Kōchi (also read Kawachi) because this was his final official post.

2. There is some controversy over the meaning of *tsuboya;* "storage shed" seems a reasonable guess.

3. Mount Mitake is another name for Kinpusan in Yoshino, center of the esoteric school of Buddhism known as Shugendō.

Chapter Twenty-Six

9. HOW MEN OF KAGA PROVINCE WHO WENT TO AN ISLAND WHERE A SNAKE WAS WARRING WITH A CENTIPEDE AIDED THE SNAKE AND SETTLED IN THE ISLAND

AT A TIME NOW PAST, there lived in —— District of Kaga Province[1] seven men of humble birth who always went to sea as a group. They liked fishing and earned their living by it. For many years all seven rowed out together in the same boat. Even though they went to fish, all were armed with bows and arrows and other weapons.

They had rowed far out, until the shore they had left behind could no longer be seen, when suddenly, without warning, fierce winds sprang up and carried them out toward the open sea. Borne along on the water, powerless to resist, they shipped their oars and entrusted themselves to the winds, bewailing their lot and expecting at every moment to die. Far ahead they caught sight of a large island, alone in the midst of the sea. Yes, they thought, an island — and if somehow they could manage to reach it, they might save themselves, if only for a time. Their ship was drawn to the island as though someone or something was pulling it in. "For the present our lives are spared," they thought, and in their joy they tumbled pell-mell out of the boat. They dragged it up onto the shore and examined the island. There were streams, and it seemed likely that there would be fruit trees. Just as they were about to go in search of something to eat, a handsome young man, apparently in his twenties, strode into view.

Here was a pleasant surprise. "So the island's inhabited!" thought the fishermen. The young man came up to them and said, "Do you know that I have brought you here as my guests?" "No," said the fishermen, "we went out to fish, but without warning were blown out to sea. To our great joy we caught sight of this island and landed here." "The wind that blew you to sea was my doing," said the man. At this they realized that he was no ordinary human being.

The battle between the centipede and the snake.

"You must be exhausted," said the man. He turned and cried loudly, "Bring the things here!" There was a sound of many feet approaching, and then two long chests were brought in,[2] as well as jars of saké in plenty. When the chests were opened the fishermen saw that they were full of delicacies. Everything was taken out and given them to eat, and they fell to heartily, for they were famished after their long day; and they drank their fill. What was left over was returned to the chests untouched, to provide for the following day, and the chests were laid aside. The bearers of the chests all departed.

Afterwards the host came up to them and said, "There is a reason why I have brought you here. Out to sea beyond this island is yet another island. Its master constantly comes here and wars against me; he wants to kill me and take possession of this island. I contrive each time to beat him back, and thus it has been for years. Tomorrow he will come again, and that day will decide which of us will live and which will die. I have asked you here with the wish that you might aid me."

The fishermen said, "How large an army will he come with? How many ships do they have? We may not be able to withstand them, but since you have brought us here in this way, we will do your bidding even it it costs us our lives."

The man showed great joy at their reply. "The enemy who is about to come is not of human shape; nor am I who prepare to meet him of human shape. Tomorrow you will see. On the previous occasions when he has tried to invade the island, I have come down on him from this higher ground. Until now I have never let my enemy come up to the foot of the waterfall; always I have driven him back at the water's edge. Tomorrow, however, I will be relying strongly on you, and therefore I will let him make his way up onto dry land. As he climbs he will gain strength, take encouragement, and advance. Leave the fighting to me for a time. If I get into difficulties, I'll make a sign with my eyes—and then you must shoot every arrow you have. Take care, whatever you do! Tomorrow morning at the Hour of the Snake[3] I will make ready, and at the Hour of the Sheep the battle will begin. Eat well, and then station yourselves on top of these cliffs. Here is where he will start his ascent." He gave them thorough instructions and then returned to the interior of the island.

The fishermen felled trees on a mountain peak and built a hut.

They sharpened their arrows and tested their bowstrings; that evening they lit a fire, and talked and made ready even as day broke. They ate their fill, and soon it was the Hour of the Snake.

As they peered into the distance they saw that a strong wind was blowing in the direction from which the enemy was to come; there was something strange and frightening about the surface of the sea. The water turned [green][4] and seemed to glow; and then out of the sea came two balls of fire. What could this be, they wondered. They turned their gaze toward the direction from which their host was to emerge to meet the enemy and saw that the mountain, too, had taken on an uncanny and frightening appearance. The grass was swaying; leaves quaked. Amidst roars of abuse, two more balls of fire came forth. As the thing from the sea swam ever closer, they saw that it was a centipede, ten yards long. Its back glowed [green]; its sides glowed scarlet. Above them on the island they saw a snake equally long, its body a full span around, descending toward the shore. Flicking its tongue, it came to confront the intruder. Who could say which of these creatures was the more fearsome! Exactly as the men had been told, the snake gave its enemy room to advance. Seeing it stop with up-raised head, the centipede took encouragement and ran up onto the land. For a time the contenders rested and waited, watching each other with angry eyes.

The seven men climbed up the cliffs as they had been instructed and fitted arrows into their bows and waited, keeping a close watch on the snake. The centipede advanced upon it at a run and sank its teeth into it. Both creatures bit each other and held fast, so that their raw flesh was covered with blood. The centipede, being a creature with many hands, [held on tight] as it bit and usually had the "upper hand."[5] After four hours[6] the snake showed signs of weakening a little. It gave the fishermen a look. "Hurry and shoot," it seemed to be thinking. The seven approached and shot every arrow they had into the centipede's entire body, from head to tail. The arrows struck so hard they were buried up to their notches. Next, the men used their swords to hack off the centipede's hands, so that it toppled onto the ground. The snake removed itself, whereupon with renewed vigor they hacked the centipede to death. The snake then went back into the interior of the island.

After some time the man whom they had seen previously reappeared. He was limping and seemed to be suffering great pain. There were wounds still bleeding on his face and neck. Again he had food and drink brought out for the men; and he expressed unbounded joy. The men cut the centipede into little bits. They made a bonfire with trees cut from the mountain and burned them in it. The bones and ashes they cast far away.

Then the man said to the fishermen, "It is thanks to you that I shall possess this island in peace. On this island there are many places that can be tilled as ricefields, and also dry fields in abundance, and countless fruit trees; it will yield rich sustenance in every way. I have it in mind to propose that you settle here. What would you say to that?"

"We would like nothing better," said the fishermen. "But what about our wives and children?"

"Go fetch them."

"But how shall we bring them across the sea?" the fishermen asked.

The man said, "When you cross to the mainland I will make the winds blow from the island. And as for your coming here: the shrine called Kumada-no-miya in Kaga Province is my subsidiary dwelling.[7] When you want to come, worship at that shrine, and you will make the crossing easily." He gave them thorough instruction, put provisions for the journey in their boat, and sent them forth. A fresh breeze sprang up from the island, and in the briefest time imaginable they had speeded across the sea.

Each of the seven men returned to his home. Inviting all those who would go to that island to accompany them, they set out in secret. They outfitted seven boats, filling them with all the different kinds of seeds they would require. They went first to the Kumada shrine and reported to the god. After they embarked, the winds sprang up again, and all seven boats crossed the sea and reached the island.

Afterwards, the seven made their homes on the island. They farmed and prospered, and their numbers increased. They are there even today. The name of the island is Cat Island.[8] Once each year the inhabitants cross the sea to Kaga Province and worship at the Kumada shrine. The people of the province know about this and watch for them but have never caught a glimpse of them. They come in the middle of the night when they are least expected, perform their ceremony, and depart; it is only afterwards that others realize that it has taken place. The ceremony has been performed annually without interruption to the present day. The island in question can be seen distinctly from a place called Ōmiya in the —— district of Noto Province. If you look far off on a clear day, you can just make out its western eminence, blue in the distance.

In the bygone era of ——, in Noto Province, there was a ship's captain named —— no Tsunemitsu. He went to this island when he was blown out to sea. The inhabitants came out and would not allow him to land. They let him moor his boat for a time by the shore and gave him provisions. Within seven or eight days a wind sprang up from the island, whereupon his boat raced swiftly back to Noto Province.

Afterwards he said, "Far off in the distance row upon row of dwellings and streets like the lanes of the capital[9] were faintly visible, and there was much traffic to and fro." Very likely it was to prevent him from observing the island more closely that they would not let him land.

In recent times, when Chinese sailors come from afar they first call at that island to take on provisions and catch fish and abalone. From there they set out for the port of Tsuruga on the mainland. In like manner, these Chinese have been forbidden to tell anyone that such an island exists.

Now think: it must surely have been owing to karma from their previous lives that these seven men settled on the island where their descendants are living even today. A happy island it is indeed! So the tale's been told, and so it's been handed down.

Notes to Story 9

1. Together with Noto Province, Kaga forms modern Ishikawa prefecture, on the Japan sea. In this story, contrary to my usual practice, I have not attempted to bridge lacunae where the compiler had intended to supply place names. In some ways this is the point of the story; it pretends to give the particulars of the origin of a real settlement, but where the settlement is and where exactly the settlers came from, the compiler does not know!

2. The text gives no hint as to who the bearers might be.

3. Nine to eleven in the morning; by Western methods of counting time, a two-hour period. Elsewhere I have converted Japanese hours

into Western units of time. Is the choice of the hour of this name coincidental? The Hour of the Sheep is from 11 A.M. to 1 P.M.

4. Lacuna in the original; one in an identical context appears a few lines lower (also in brackets). "Green" is the suggestion of several commentators.

5. In Japanese as well as English the centipede's appendages are called feet, but the author was preparing the somewhat feeble pun here.

6. Four Western hours; see note 3 above.

7. This shrine, in Kumada-mura, is mentioned in the *Engi-shiki*; it was moved in the seventeenth century on account of floods and seems no longer to exist. With this speech the man identifies himself — were there any doubt about it — as a Shinto god.

8. The name of Cat Island (Neko no shima) no longer exists, but commentators identify the island with Hegurajima. It is curious that the legend makes no attempt to explain the name.

9. The *kōji* of Kyoto were approximately forty feet across.

Chapter Twenty-Seven

15. HOW A WOMAN WHO WAS BEARING A CHILD WENT TO SOUTH YAMASHINA, ENCOUNTERED AN ONI, AND ESCAPED

AT A TIME NOW PAST, there was a young woman who was in service at a certain great house. She had neither parents nor relatives and no real friends, so that she had nowhere to turn in case of need. She never ventured from her chamber. Who would take care of her if she fell ill, she wondered anxiously; and then she found herself pregnant without a proper husband.

The more she pondered her fate, the more unrelieved was her misery. The first necessity was to find a place to give birth. She did not know what to do, and there was no one to advise her. She thought about speaking to her master, but she was ashamed to confess her condition.

She was an intelligent woman nonetheless, and an idea occurred to her. "When I feel the first signs of approaching birth, I will go away by myself, with only my serving girl as a companion. It doesn't matter where I go, so long as it is deep in the mountains. I'll find a tree and give birth under it. If I die, no one will ever know, and that will be the end of it. If I survive, I will return here and pretend that nothing has happened." The month gradually drew near. She was unspeakably wretched, but she behaved as though nothing were amiss. Secretly she made preparations, readying a small store of food and giving instructions to her young maid. Soon her time was at hand.

She felt the first signs before dawn. Anxious to be gone before it was light, she had the girl gather up the provisions and hurried with her from the house. The mountains must lie close by the eastern boundaries of the capital, she thought, and set out eastward; but daybreak found her no farther than the Kamo River bank. Where could she go now? But she summoned up her courage and, halting often to rest, walked on toward Awatayama[1] and entered into the deep forest. She walked about looking for a suitable spot until she came to an area called North Yamashina.[2]

Nestled among the cliffs were the remains of an ancient mountain estate. The house itself had long since gone to ruin. There
was no sign of human habitation. Here, she decided, she would
give birth, and here she would abandon her child. There was a
wall, but she managed to climb over it.

Here and there in the guest wing were places where the floor
was still sound. She had sat down at the edge of the veranda to rest
when she heard someone approaching from an inner room. "So
someone lives here after all!" she thought in misery. A door slid
open and a white-haired old woman came out. "Surely she'll
scold me and order me away," she thought, but the old woman
smiled benignly.

"Who is it that pays me this unexpected call?" said the old
woman. Amidst tears the young woman told her her story. "You
poor thing!" the old woman said, "you shall have your baby
here," and called her in. The young woman was overjoyed. The
Buddha had come to her aid, she thought. Within, a simple bed
was prepared for her, and not long afterwards she had an easy
delivery.

The old woman came to her and said, "My best congratulations! Old people like me who live in countrified places like this
don't need to worry about taboos. Why don't you stay here for
seven days, until your defilement is over." She had the serving
girl heat water to wash the newborn. The mother was happy. The
infant was a beautiful little boy; she could never abandon it now,
and she lay there nursing it.

A few days later, as she was taking an afternoon nap with the
infant beside her, she heard ever so faintly the old woman say,
"Only a mouthful, but my how delicious!" She opened her eyes
to see the old woman gazing at the child intently and was terrified. "She is an oni," the young woman thought, "and she will
devour us." She knew that somehow or other she must steal
away.

There came the time when the old woman took a long afternoon nap. The mother stealthily put the infant on the servant-
girl's back and, lightly dressed, left the house and ran back down
the road she had come as fast as her legs would carry her. "Buddha save me!" she prayed. Soon they were at Awataguchi. From
there she went to the Kamo River bank, where she stopped at a
humble cottage and set her appearance to rights. After sundown

she returned to the house of her master. It was her quick-wittedness that saved her. The child she entrusted to a nurse.

What became of the old woman after that no one knows. The young woman said nothing to anyone of what she had experienced. It was only after she herself had grown old that she told her story.

Now think: ancient places of that sort always have supernatural beings living in them. "Only a mouthful, but my how delicious!" Only an oni could have looked at an infant and said that.

This shows that you should never go into such places alone. So the tale's been told, and so it's been handed down.

Notes to Story 15

---

1. At the northern entrance to Higashiyama, a hilly area to the south and east of the original boundaries of Kyoto.

2. South Yamashina, in the title of the story, seems to be a copyist's slip. North Yamashina corresponds to the area of the same name in the eastern part of Higashiyama-ku of modern Kyoto.

22. HOW THE HUNTERS' MOTHER BECAME AN ONI AND TRIED TO DEVOUR HER CHILDREN

AT A TIME NOW PAST, in a district and province [the names of which are no longer known], there were two brothers who got their livelihood by killing deer and boar. They went into the mountains regularly to shoot deer, so that elder and younger brother went as a team.

They hunted by a technique called "waiting." They would lash pieces of wood high across the cleft of some great tree and sit down to wait; when deer passed underneath they would shoot. The brothers were sitting in the trees about fifty or sixty yards apart, facing each other. It was a moonless night toward the end of the ninth month, so dark that not a thing could be seen. They waited in hopes of hearing deer come, but night gradually deepened and there were none.

Now, as the elder brother was sitting in his tree the hand of some supernatural being reached down from above, seized his topknot, and began to draw him upward. Alarmed, he felt for the hand: it was the hand of a human being, emaciated and withered. "An oni has gotten hold of me and is pulling me upward in order to eat me — that must be the explanation," he thought. He would tell his brother sitting opposite, he decided. He shouted to him, and there was an answering shout.

The elder brother said, "Suppose just now some weird creature had taken hold of my topknot and were pulling me upwards: what would you do?"

"I'd figure out where it is and shoot it," the younger said.

The older said, "It's true. Something really has taken hold of my topknot just now and is pulling me upwards."

"I'll aim by your voice," the younger said.

"Well then, shoot," said the elder, and accordingly the younger let fly a forked arrow. He sensed that it had struck just above his brother's head. "It seems to me I've hit it," he said. The elder brother felt above his head and found that the hand that had seized him had been severed at the wrist and was dangling. He took it and said, "You've already cut off the hand that took hold of me; I have it here. Let's call it a night and go home."

"All right," said the younger. Both came down from their trees, and they went home together. It was well past midnight when they got back.

Now they had an aged mother, so infirm that she could scarcely get about. They had set up quarters for her in a tiny house of her own; their own houses stood on either side so they could keep an eye on her. Upon returning from the mountains they heard her moaning strangely. "Why are you moaning, Mother?" they asked, but she made no reply. They then lit torches and together examined the severed hand; it resembled their mother's hand. Horrified, they examined it closely: it could be no other. They opened the sliding door to their mother's room, and she rose to her feet. "You — you —" she said and started to lunge at them. "Is this your hand, madam?" they said, threw it inside, slid the door shut, and went away.

Not long afterwards she died. When her sons looked at her close up they saw that one of her hands was missing, severed at the wrist. So it had indeed been their mother's hand, they realized. Senile and demented, their mother had become an oni and followed her children into the mountains to devour them.

When parents become extremely old they always turn into oni and try to eat even their own children. But she was their mother and they buried her.

Now think: how fearsome it was! So the tale's been told, and so it's been handed down.

29. ABOUT THE TWO WET-NURSES IN THE HOUSE OF MIDDLE CAPTAIN MASAMICHI WHO LOOKED EXACTLY ALIKE

AT A TIME NOW PAST, there was a Middle Captain named Minamoto no Masamichi. He was known as the Tanba Middle Captain.[1] His house was situated south of Fourth Avenue and west of Muromachi.

During the time that he was living there, his son, an infant in perhaps his second year,[2] was carried in his nurse's arms to the front part[3] of the compound and left to play alone in a spot some distance from the house itself. Suddenly the child screamed in terror, and nurses were heard quarreling. The Captain was on the other side of the house, and sword in hand, he ran to see what was the matter. There were two nurses who looked exactly alike, and his son was between them. Each had grasped a hand and a foot and was trying to tug him to her.

The Captain observed them in momentary bafflement. The two wet-nurses looked exactly alike, and he did not know which was the true one. "One must surely be a fox," he thought. Brandishing his sword, he rushed upon them, whereupon one of the nurses vanished into thin air.

Both the child and the nurse lay as though dead. The Captain called his servants and had exorcists summoned to perform their magic rites. After a short time the nurse came to herself and got to her feet.

"What on earth happened?" asked the Captain.

The nurse said, "While I was giving the young master his airing, a maid who was a stranger to me suddenly came out of the

Rushing upon a supernatural creature with a sword
will frighten it away.

house. 'That's my child,' she said, and grabbed him. I was tugging at him to keep her from making off with him when you ran at her with your sword. She gave up just like that and went back toward the house.'' The Captain was horrified.

That's why people say it won't do to let children play where no one's about. Whether it was a fox at its tricks or some evil spirit, no one knows. So the tale's been told, and so it's been handed down.

Notes to Story 29

1. Masamichi (d. 1017) was so called because he was governor of Tanba; among the texts in which he appears is the *Murasaki Shikibu nikki.*

2. By Japanese count; perhaps a year old by Western count.

3. Literally, on the south side: houses faced south.

41. HOW THE FOX OF KŌYAGAWA TURNED INTO A WOMAN AND RODE ON HORSES' CROUPS

AT A TIME NOW PAST, there was east of the temple Ninnaji a river called Kōyagawa,[1] and on its banks toward sundown a pretty young girl would be standing. Whenever someone passed by on horseback on his way to the capital she would say, "I'd like to go to the capital. Let me ride behind you, on the croup of your horse." "Get on," the rider would say, and lift her on, but after she had ridden four or five hundred yards she would suddenly leap down from the horse and take to her heels, and when the rider chased her she would change into a fox and run from sight, barking shrilly.

Such incidents took place repeatedly and became a popular topic of conversation. One day a number of the guards attached to the Sovereign's Private Office were gathered in their palace head-quarters chatting about one thing and the next. Someone brought up the story of the girl at Kōyagawa who rode on horses' croups. One of the guards, a young man of fierce courage and keen judg-ment, said, "Now if it were I—I'd catch that girl and truss her up.

Those people were stupid to let her escape." The other guards were in high spirits. "You'll never do it!" they said. The one who had said he would catch her replied, "Just for that, tomorrow night I'll tie her up and bring her here with me." The others remained unconvinced. "You can't," they said, and the argument flew back and forth.

The next evening, mounted on a fine horse and completely unattended, the guard went to Kōyagawa. As he crossed the river the girl was nowhere to be seen. He turned around immediately. As he was riding back toward the capital the girl was standing there. She saw him pass and said with a smile, "Please, sir, let me ride on the croup of your horse." She spoke prettily and looked altogether charming. "Hurry and get on," the guardsman said. "Where are you going?" he asked. The girl said, "I'm going up to the capital, but it's past sundown, so I'd like to ride there on the croup of your horse." He lifted her on forthwith, and as he did so he took a bridle rope which he had prepared in advance and lashed her to the saddle. "What are you doing this for?" she asked.

"Now that we're traveling together, I'm going to sleep with you in my arms tonight," he replied. "It wouldn't do for you to run away, would it." They rode along together. It was already completely dark.

He galloped eastward down First Avenue. Just as he was passing Ōmiya West, he saw coming toward him from the east a long line of torches. The carriages came one after another, outriders shouting to clear the way before them. This was obviously the procession of some grand personage, the guard thought, so he wheeled around, went south on Ōmiya West to Second Avenue, east on Second Avenue to Ōmiya East, and thence north to Tsuchimikado. He had told his attendants to await him at the gate. "Men, are you there?" he called. "All here," came the reply, and some ten men came out.

Then he loosened the cord with which he had tied the girl and pulled her down from the horse; seizing the miscreant by the arm he went in through the gate, preceded by torches. He took her to the guards' headquarters. The guards were all sitting in a row, waiting. "How did it go?" they cried. "Here she is, all tied up," he answered. The girl was crying. "Let me go now, please!" she said. "Why are all these people here?"

Ignoring her misery, he dragged her along. The guardsmen

stood up and formed a circle around her, torches blazing. "Turn her loose inside the circle," they said. "I can't do that. She'll run away," he said. They fitted arrows to their bows. "Turn her loose and we'll have some fun. Let's shoot at the scamp's haunches. If we were just one man, we might miss, but . . ." There were ten of them, taking aim, ready to shoot. "All right," he said, and suddenly released her. At that moment the girl changed into a fox and ran away barking shrilly. The circle of guardsmen vanished on the spot. The torches had gone out and it was pitch dark.

Bewildered, the guard shouted for his followers, but not a one was there. Looking about him, he saw that he was out in the fields — but in what place he hadn't the faintest notion. His heart was pounding and he was choking with fear. Feeling as though he were scarcely alive he summoned his wits and examined his surroundings at length. From the height of the mountains and the shape of the terrain he realized that he was in the cremation grounds at Toribeno. He thought he had got down from his horse at Tsuchimikado.[2] But where then was his horse? "Why, I must have come here when I thought I was going around the palace enclosure from Ōmiya West! The torchlight procession that I met on First Avenue was a trick of the fox," he thought. Since he could hardly remain there, he slowly returned home on foot. It was midnight when he reached his house.

The next day he was confused in mind and distraught and lay as though dead. The guards had waited for him the night before, and when he did not appear they laughed and said to each other, "Whatever became of that fellow who said he'd tie up the fox of Kōyagawa?" They sent a messenger to summon him. Toward evening three days later he came to the headquarters, looking as though he had been deathly ill. "What happened with the fox the other night?" the guardsmen asked him. "That evening I came down with a painful illness," he said, "and wasn't able to go. But I'll give it a try tonight." The other guardsmen made fun of him. "This time bring back two," they said, laughing, and he strode out with few words.

He thought to himself, "Because she was tricked the first time, the fox surely will not appear tonight. And if she does come — I'll have to watch her the whole night through, for if I let go of her she'll escape. But if she doesn't come I'll never show my face in the guard room again; I'll become a hermit." The same evening, accompanied by a number of brawny followers, he got on a horse and rode to Kōyagawa. "I'm just throwing my life away," he thought, but since he had brought the dare on himself, he had to go through with it.

He did not see her as he crossed the Kōyagawa, but when he turned to ride back, a young girl was standing on the river bank. Her face was different from the previous girl's. Just as before, she said, "Let me ride on your horse's croup," and he lifted her on. Just as before he lashed her down with a bridle rope and returned to the capital with her tightly bound, proceeding down First Avenue. Since it was dark now, he had some of his attendants go ahead of him with torches while others stayed close beside his horse. Shouting to clear the way, they went along in orderly fashion and met no one. At Tsuchimikado he got down from his horse, seized the girl by the hair, and dragged her to the guard room. All the way there she cried and begged to be let go.

"What's this? What's this?" said the guardsmen. "Here she is," he said, and this time he kept her tightly bound. She remained a human being for a little while, but after they tortured her she became a fox. The guardsmen burned her hair off with pine torches and shot at her again and again. "No more of your tricks from now on, you hear?" they said, and let her go without killing her. Although she was unable to walk, she managed with much effort to make her escape. And then the guard recounted in detail how previously he had been tricked and gone to Toribeno.

Ten days or so later the guard rode to Kōyagawa thinking he would try again. There she was, the same girl as before, standing on the river bank, but she looked as though she had been deathly ill. As he had before, he spoke to her. "Well, little dear, come ride on the croup of my horse."

"I'd like to ride," the girl said. "But sir! When you burn me I can't bear it," and she vanished.

The fox paid very dearly for trying to trick people. The affair is supposed to have taken place not long ago. Since it's a queer tale it was told and passed on.

Now think: there's nothing unusual in a fox taking human form; it's happened often since ancient times. But what an impudent trick it was, to take him all the way to Toribeno! And then why was it that on the second occasion the guardsman did not see the procession or lose his way? Some have guessed that how a fox behaves depends on the person's state of mind. So the tale's been told, and so it's been handed down.

Notes to Story 41

1. The Kōyagawa arises at Takagamine, in the northern part of Kyoto.

2. The place from which he was returning was to the west of the capital. The guards' headquarters was inside the greater imperial palace enclosure, which was situated at the northern end of the city, theoretically midway between east and west. Major east-west avenues were numbered from the northern boundary of the city, with First Avenue the northern boundary also of the imperial enclosure. The two north-south streets that bound the enclosure on the west and east were named Ōmiya West and Ōmiya East. The palace enclosure had numerous gates, of which Jōtōmon, on the avenue called Tsuchimikado, was at the northeast. The guardsman was being forced to make a considerable detour to get to it.

5. HOW TAMEMORI, THE GOVERNOR OF ECHIZEN, SUBDUED THE JUNIOR OFFICERS OF THE SIX COMPANIES OF THE GUARDS

AT A TIME NOW PAST, there was a man named Fujiwara no Tamemori Ason.[1] It happened that while he was governor of Echizen he failed to pay in his share of the salary rice due the Companies of the Palace Guards. Every last man of the Six Companies of the Guards[2] was angered, junior officers and men in the ranks alike. Carrying their flat-roofed tents,[3] they went to Tamemori's house and pitched them in front of his gate; they set camp stools underneath and sat down side by side in a solid row so that the inhabitants could neither enter nor leave, and there they remained, demanding their pay.

It was the sixth month, when the days are long and very hot. The Guards had been sitting there since before daybreak, and by early afternoon[4] they were dizzy from the sun and the heat. They were resolved, nevertheless, not to leave without getting what they had come for. At length, the gate of the house opened a crack and an aged retainer stuck his head out.

"His honor the Governor has asked me to speak to you on his behalf," he said. " 'I would like to meet with you in person at the earliest opportunity,' he says, 'but my wife and children are terrified and in tears owing to this extraordinary harassment, and so I am quite unable to discuss the matter with you face to face. Now, it seems to me that you have been waiting all day in this heat; surely your throats must be dry. Moreover, it's occurred to me that we might contrive to talk things over through a partition. I've been thinking: suppose I were to call you in quietly—shall we say, for refreshments? Would that suit you? If you've no objection, I'll ask the officers and men of the Left and Right Companies of the Inner Guards please to enter first. After they've left, I'll speak with you gentlemen of the other companies in turn. I ought to see you all at once, I know, but this place is so dingy and cramped, there's not room enough for a crowd. Please be patient

Tamemori looks out from behind the blinds as
Kanetoki and Atsuyuki feast; members of the other companies
of the guards continue their vigil, at the lower right.

just a little longer. Now if the Inner Guards will enter first—'
That's his message," said the retainer.

The men were utterly parched from the heat of the sun, and
they were overjoyed at the thought that now they would have the
chance to present their complaint. "How very kind of him!" they
replied. "Let's go in at once and explain what has brought us
here."

"Very well," said the retainer, whereupon the gate was opened
and the officials and men of the Left and Right Companies of the
Inner Guards all went in.

Long mats had been laid out along three sections of the north
gallery adjoining the inner gate, and on them two rows of some
twenty or thirty tables had been set up facing each other. These,
the men saw, were laden with all sorts of salty tidbits: minced
salt-dried bream, salt-pickled salmon that looked very salty indeed, salt-cured mackerel, and bream in fermented bean sauce.
For fruit there were purple plums, dead ripe, that filled ten great
Kasuga bowls[5] to overflowing. When all the food had been set
out, the retainer said, "This way please, the Inner Guards first,
please," whereupon the most venerable elderly Guards came
crowding in, with Owari no Kanetoki and Shimotsuke no Atsuyuki[6] at their head. "That's enough now," said the retainer. "The
rest of you will have to wait," and he closed the gate and locked it
and took the key.

The Guards were lined up at the inner gate, and bidden to
hasten, they went up onto the veranda and took their seats across
from one another in two long rows. "Quick, bring the wine
cups," the retainer called, but for a long time no wine came, and
meanwhile the Guards, who were famished, set to with their
chopsticks, tasting and chewing all the things cured in salt and
pickled in bean sauce, the salmon, the bream, and everything
else. "How slow the wine is!" said the retainer, but even so none
appeared. A message was brought: "The Governor feels he should
greet you, but just at the moment he's incapacitated with a ca-
tarrh, and he can't come just yet. Have some refreshments while
you're waiting, and he'll be out." Still no wine came.

And here at last was the wine. Two young attendants came,
each bearing a pair of big-bellied wine cups, which they set on
trays and put between Kanetoki and Atsuyuki, who sat facing
each other. Next they brought great pitchers brimming with

wine. Kanetoki and Atsuyuki took up their cups and let them be filled to overflowing. The wine was a little muddy and sour, they noticed, but their throats were so parched from the sun that they drank on without pause. They drained their cups three times before setting them down. The other Guards were equally thirsty and gulped down two or three, four or five cups apiece just to moisten their throats. They ate the plums as they drank, and then more wine was urged on them, so they drank a fourth or fifth, a fifth or sixth time. It was only then that the Governor crept[7] out to a seat behind the blinds.

"Gentlemen, my profoundest regrets! I never thought I would be subjected to your reproaches. Last year there was drought in my province, and I took in nothing, nothing at all. Oh, perhaps there was a grain or two of tax rice, but their eminences above squeezed that out of me. There's nothing left. There's not even food for my household. The serving girls go hungry. I can only think that fate has ordained that I should suffer this shame. Please understand that I am unable to offer you so much as a potful of rice. Thanks to the sins of my previous lives, for years I failed to be appointed to office, and when I did by chance obtain a post it was as governor to an impoverished province. For my hardships I blame no one but myself; it's all the fault of my evil karma." And he wept loudly and copiously.

Kanetoki and Atsuyuki were sitting closest to the Governor, so that the insistent rumbling that came from their stomachs was very audible to him. Rumbling and squealing: for a while they drummed their ceremonial batons against the tables to cover the sound. . . .[8] As the Governor looked on from his side of the blinds, all the stomachs rumbled in concert, and every man, down to the last table, writhed with cramps.

"Excuse me a moment," said Kanetoki, and he took off at a run. At this signal, the other Guards rose from their seats and scrambled pell-mell in his wake, jumping down from the veranda or leaping from the beams,[9] farting and crapping. Some ran to the carriage shed and began to shit before they had time to loosen their clothes. Others hiked up their garments and let it squirt.[10] Others, unable to conceal themselves, just crapped in a daze. For all that, they were laughing.

"Just as we thought, those old fellows don't fool around. We figured he'd pull something. No, we've no grudge against his lordship. We did it to ourselves with our thirst." And they all laughed as they crapped in agony.

Then the gate was opened. "Well, gentlemen, you may leave now. And would the officers of the other companies please enter."

"Splendid. Come right in and get made to crap like us."

All the men's trousers were befouled; seeing them scramble out wiping the shit off, the Guards of the other four companies ran away laughing.

In fact, it was just as Tamemori had planned. "I'll let them roast under the sun for six or eight hours, and then I'll call them in. They'll be good and thirsty. I'll give them plums and salt fish to whet their appetites, and when they've stuffed their empty stomachs with those I'll have them drink muddy sour wine and lace it with ground convolvulus seeds.[11] Won't that crowd of rascals be shitting green!"

That Tamemori was a clever one, an ingenious old dandy who loved surprises and was always making people laugh, and this was typical of him. People of the time laughed and said it was the Guards' hard luck that they went to the home of a joker.

The Guards must have learned their lesson, for they never again went in protest to the house of a provincial governor who had failed to contribute to their pay. It was the height of cleverness, not to have tried to drive them away by force but to have contrived such a prank. So the tale's been told, and so it's been handed down.

Notes to Story 5

1. Tamemori became governor of Echizen in 1028 and died in 1029. Echizen was in the far north of Japan, but the incident takes place while he is in his residence in Kyoto.

2. Six Companies of the Guards: *rokuefu*, the guards who protected the imperial palace (not to be confused with, e.g., the *takiguchi*, guards attached to the Sovereign's Private Office, who appear in 27:41). These companies were the Inner Palace Guards, Right and Left Divisions; the Middle Palace Guards, Right and Left Divisions; and the Outer Palace Guards, Right and Left Divisions. Junior officers renders *kannin*, officials of the rank of *shōgen* ("Lieutenant") and below.

3. Flat-roofed tents: *hirabari*, a kind of portable awning used for protection from light rain or the direct rays of the sun and suitable for little more.

4. Literally, the Hour of the Sheep: see 26:9, note 3.

5. Bowls lacquered red on the outside and black on the inside, ornamented with mother-of-pearl and the like, a product of Nara.

6. There are numerous other mentions of Kanetoki and Atsuyuki in *Konjaku*; a translation of 23:26, which tells of a contest in horsemanship in which the vanquished man acquitted himself with even more distinction than the victor, appears in Frank, pp. 156–157. Kanetoki was appointed Lieutenant of the Inner Palace Guards, Left Division, in 998.

7. Not out of humility but because this was a normal method of locomotion when only a short distance needed to be traversed indoors.

8. Ellipsis points represent a brief passage that is unintelligible and may be corrupt; one possible interpretation is "their fists dug grooves in the mats."

9. Beams: *nageshi,* long, narrow beams laid on the floor, which divided the outer from the inner veranda.

10. Literally, "like water from a *hanzō.*" A *hanzō* was a jug outfitted with a mechanism to spray water. The *Konjaku* compiler was fond of this simile and used it also in 19:18, which relates among the eccentricities of the monk Zōga his yielding to an attack of diarrhea all too shortly after ordaining an empress dowager.

11. It may be superfluous to remark that seeds of the convolvulus were a common laxative. See F. Porter Stuart, *Chinese Materia Medica* (Shanghai, 1911), pp. 489–490, under *Ipomoea hederacea.*

11. HOW KAISHU, THE INTENDANT OF GION, WAS GIVEN AS A FEE FOR CHANTING THE SUTRAS

AT A TIME NOW PAST, there was an intendant of Gion named Kaishu,[1] a senior monk of the imperial temple, who made illicit visits to the house of a certain prominent deputy governor. The deputy governor had a notion that something was going on but pretended to know nothing. One day when Kaishu had taken advantage of his absence to come there and was lording it about and looking very smug, the Governor returned. The mistress of the house and her maids seemed strangely flustered, and the Governor thought to himself, "Aha! just as I suspected!" He went into the interior of the house and saw that a clothes chest[2] ordinarily left open was locked. "No doubt about it. They put him in there and turned the key." He summoned a senior retainer and called for two porters. "Take this chest to Gion at once and give it to the monks as a fee for chanting sutras," he said. He gave the retainer a letter to carry, folded in the formal style. The chest was dragged out and given to the retainer, who had the porters hoist it onto their shoulders, and away they went. The wife and her maids were horrified but in their astonishment said not a word.

When the retainer arrived at Gion with the chest, all the monks came out to view the treasure they were sure it must contain. "Run and tell the intendant," they said to one of their number. "We can't open this until he comes." They waited expectantly while the man went off to notify the intendant. After a long time he returned and said, "I can't find the intendant anywhere." The retainer sent to order the chanting of the sutras said, "I can't go on waiting. As I myself am present, no one will accuse you of dishonesty if you open the chest. But do it now. I'm in a hurry."

"Can that be proper?" The monks debated, unable to make up their minds.

From within the chest came a wee, mournful voice. "You don't need the intendant; the rector will do." Upon hearing this, monks and messenger alike were flabbergasted. But things couldn't be left as they were, and ever so fearfully they opened the chest. While they watched, the intendant poked his head out. The monks all fled with eyes and mouths agape; the Governor's messenger, too, took to his heels and returned home. As for the intendant, he emerged from the chest and went into hiding.

Now think: the Governor would have liked to drag Kaishu from the chest and give him a good kicking, but he thought how painful it would be if the affair became known. Instead he decided to shame him. How astute he was! Kaishu for his part was known for his ready tongue, and he used it even inside the chest. When the tale got out he was praised for his quick-wittedness. So the tale's been told, and so it's been handed down.

Notes to Story 11

1. Gion is an abbreviation of Gionsha, an old name for the Yasaka shrine. This Shinto shrine was originally established as a Buddhist

temple. An intendant *(bettō)* was in charge of a temple, placed there as representative of the imperial government. Kaishu's name is written variously in different texts and (depending on the characters) might also be read Kanjū, Kanshu. It has been suggested that he was a half-brother of Sei Shōnagon, author of the Pillow Book.

2. Clothes chest: *karabitsu,* literally Cathay chest, a large trunk with four legs and a lid, used to store clothes and bedding.

38. HOW FUJIWARA NO NOBUTADA, GOVERNOR OF SHINANO, TOOK A TUMBLE AT MISAKA

AT A TIME NOW PAST, there was a man named Fujiwara no Nobutada who was governor of Shinano.[1] He had journeyed to Shinano upon his appointment and, having served his term, was returning to the capital. He rode in the midst of a long procession, packhorses loaded with his goods, his retainers (more men than you could count) on horseback. As he was crossing the suspension bridge at Misaka[2] his horse caught a hind foot on a plank at the rim and slipped and fell. Horse and rider together went tumbling head over heels into the ravine.

The ravine was immeasurably deep, and it seemed therefore scarcely likely that the Governor could still be alive. Far below could be seen the topmost branches of hundred-foot cypresses and cedars, but try as they might, none of his men could tell how much farther it was to the ground. No, they thought, there was not the faintest chance that the Governor could be unharmed after such a fall. They all dismounted and, kneeling in a row at the rim of the bridge, peered helplessly into the depths.

"It's hopeless. If only there were somewhere not too steep, so we could climb down and find out what has happened to him. We'll have to go on for another day and circle back from the shallow end to look for him. There's no way at all to get down here." One after another, all were exclaiming in dismay. And then faintly, from far below, a shout was heard.

"That was his lordship the Governor," they said, and gave an answering yell. By listening intently they could just make out his words.

"He's telling us something. Listen everyone! What is it?"

Nobutada, mushrooms in hand, in the travel hamper.

"He says we're to let down a travel hamper[3] on a long rope."

They knew now that the Governor was alive: something had broken his fall. A great many men collected their reins, tied them end to end and fastened them to the hamper, which they lowered in all haste. The rope was paid out until none was left; only then did it begin to go slack. It must have hit bottom, they thought.

From the depths of the ravine came the voice: "Now pull it up."

"He's telling us to pull," they said.

The hamper seemed extraordinarily light as they reeled it up.

"How light it is! Surely it should be heavier if the Governor is in it," they said. "It must be that he's catching hold of branches as he rises," someone suggested.

All pulled together. When they had drawn the basket all the way up they saw that it held nothing but mushrooms. They stared into each other's faces uncomprehendingly. "What on earth?" they said.

Once more a shout was heard from below. "All right, let it down again." And so they did. Again they heard the shout to pull it up. They obeyed, and this time the hamper was extremely heavy. Many men heaved at the rope to reel it in. This time indeed the Governor was riding in the hamper. With one hand he was clutching the rope; in the other he carried three clusters of mushrooms. He was hoisted up and set down on the bridge amidst general rejoicing.

"Sir, are these some special kind of mushroom?" the retainers asked him.

The Governor replied, "At the time of the fall, my horse went straight down to the bottom of the ravine. I felt myself spinning through the air after him when, unexpectedly, I fell into a dense tangle of branches. I grabbed at them until I came to rest against a large branch below. Using it as a foothold, I made my way to the fork of the tree and stayed there with my arms around the trunk. So many mushrooms are growing on that tree that I couldn't take my eyes off them. I took just the ones within easy reach and had you haul them up in the hamper. But there must be a lot left — more than I know how to say, in fact. It's a terrible loss, a terrible loss, and I feel it keenly."

"Oh, indeed, sir, a great loss," said the retainers, and burst out laughing together.

"Don't talk nonsense," said the Governor. "You fellows are the kind who would climb a mountain of jewels and come back empty-handed, I can see that. You know the saying: a governor can't stumble without snatching a handful of dirt."

His senior deputy was inwardly repelled but said, "Right you are, sir. How could you fail to take whatever might come into your hands? It might be expected of anyone. But only a man endowed with your innate sagacity would carry on unperturbed in the face of death and pick mushrooms quite as though nothing were in the least amiss. You govern your province with the same wisdom, garnering taxes and enriching yourself to your heart's content: that's why the people of the province love and cherish you like a parent. And so, sir, what can we do but congratulate you." The speech went on and on as the others secretly burst into guffaws.

Now think: such was the Governor's greed that even in straits like these his first thought was for the mushrooms: he picked them and sent them up without a tremor of fear. You can imagine, therefore, what he was like when the opportunities for gain were easier. How people who heard this must have detested him—and how they must have laughed! So the tale's been told, and so it's been handed down.

Notes to Story 38

1. Shinano is modern Nagano prefecture. Nobutada was appointed governor in 982, and his successor was appointed in the spring of 988, so it seems likely that this incident took place in 988.

2. Kamisaka Pass, a renowned danger spot on the border between ancient Shinano and Mino provinces.

3. Travel hamper: *hatago,* large baskets used to carry fodder for horses.

Chapter Twenty-Nine

18. HOW A THIEF CLIMBED
TO THE UPPER STORY OF RASHŌ GATE
AND SAW A CORPSE

AT A TIME NOW PAST, there was a man who had come to the capital from the direction of Settsu Province[1] in order to steal. The sun was still high, so he concealed himself beneath Rashō gate.[2] Shujaku Avenue, to the north, was thronged, and he stood there waiting for the street to become quiet; but then as he waited he heard a great many people approaching from the other direction, and to avoid being seen by them he climbed silently to the upper story. There he saw the faint light of a torch.

This was strange, the thief thought, and he peered through the lattices. A young woman was lying dead. A torch had been lit at her pillow, and beside it sat a white-haired crone who was plucking and tearing the hair from the corpse's head.

The thief saw but could not comprehend. Could these be oni? he wondered. He was afraid, but he thought, "They may only be ghosts. I'll try scaring them off." He quietly opened the door and drew his sword. "You there, you there," he cried, and rushed in upon them.

The crone cowered in confusion and rubbed her hands together. "Who are you, old woman, and what are you doing here?" the thief asked.

"I lost my mistress, sir," she said, "and as there was no one to bury her, I brought her here. See what nice long hair she has. I'm plucking it out to make a wig. Spare me!"

The thief stripped the corpse and the old woman of the clothes they wore and stole the hair. He ran to the ground and made his getaway.

There used to be a lot of corpses in the upper story of that gate. It's a fact that when people died and for some reason or other couldn't be buried they were brought there.

The thief told someone what had happened, and whoever heard his story passed it on. So the tale's been told, and so it's been handed down.

Notes to Story 18

---

1. That is, from the south. (Settsu is part of modern Hyōgo prefecture.)

2. See 24:24, note 2.

23. HOW A MAN WHO WAS ACCOMPANYING HIS WIFE TO TANBA PROVINCE GOT TRUSSED UP AT ŌEYAMA

AT A TIME NOW PAST, a man who lived in the capital had a wife who came from Tanba Province.[1] He accompanied her on a journey to Tanba. The husband had his wife ride their horse, while he himself walked along behind, keeping guard, with a quiver with ten arrows on his back and a bow in his hand. Not far from Ōeyama there fell in with them a brawny-looking young man with a sword at his waist.

They walked along together, each inquiring politely where the other was going and chatting about this and that. The new man, the one with the sword, said, "This is a famous sword that I'm wearing, an heirloom from Mutsu Province. Look at it," and he unsheathed it. In truth it was a magnificent blade, and when the husband saw it he wanted it above all things. The new man saw the expression on his face and said, "Do you want this sword? I'll trade it for that bow you're carrying." The man with the bow knew his bow to be of no great value, while the sword was exceptionally fine. What with his desire for the sword and his greed for a profitable bargain, he made the exchange without a second thought.

Well then, as they were walking on the new man said, "I look ridiculous carrying a bow and nothing else. While we're in the mountains lend me a couple of arrows. After all, sir, we're traveling together, so it's all the same where you're concerned."

To the first man this seemed reasonable enough. He was in high good humor at having exchanged his worthless bow for a valuable sword, and so he took out two arrows and handed them over as he'd been asked. The new man walked behind, the bow and two arrows ready in his grasp. The first man walked ahead, with the sword at his waist and the useless quiver on his back.

After a time the travelers went into a grove to have their afternoon meal. The new man said, "It's not nice to eat where people can see. Let's go on a little," and so they went deep into the trees. Then, just as the husband had put his arms around his wife to lift her from the horse, the other man suddenly fitted an arrow to his bow, aimed at him, and pulled it taut. "I'll shoot if you move," he said.

The first man hadn't expected anything at all like this and stood looking at him dumbfounded. The other threatened him. "Go on into the mountains, go on!" Afraid for his life, he went with his wife perhaps half a mile further into the mountains. "Throw away your sword and knife," the other commanded, and he threw them away. The other man approached, picked them up and knocked him down, and tied him fast to a tree with the bridle rope.

Then this man went up to the woman and looked at her closely. She was twenty or a little older, and of humble station but adorably pretty. Her beauty aroused his desire, and forgetting any other purpose, he made her take off her clothes. The woman had no way of resisting, and so she stripped as he told her to. Then he too undressed and embraced her and lay with her. The woman was helpless and had to obey. All the while her husband watched in his trusses. What must he have thought!

Afterwards, the man arose, dressed himself as before, strapped the quiver on his back and the sword to his waist and, bow in hand, hoisted himself onto the horse. To the woman he said, "I'm sorry, but I must go away. I have no choice. As a favor to you I'll spare your husband's life. I'm taking the horse so I can make a quick escape." And he galloped away, no one knows where.

After that, the wife went up to her husband and freed his bonds. He looked stupefied. "You wretch!" she exclaimed. "You good-for-nothing coward! From this day forward I'll never trust you again." Her husband said not a word, and together they went to Tanba.

The rapist had a sense of shame, for after all he did not rob the woman of her clothes. But the husband was a worthless fool: in the mountains to hand his bow and arrows to someone he'd never before laid eyes on was surely the height of stupidity.

No one knows what became of the other man. So the tale goes, and so it's been handed down.

Note to Story 23

---

1. To the west of the capital; now lying chiefly within the western portion of Kyoto prefecture.

28. HOW A BEGGAR WHO LIVED IN THE AREA SOUTH OF KIYOMIZU USED A WOMAN TO LURE MEN INTO HIS HOUSE AND KILLED THEM

AT A TIME NOW PAST, there was a man of noble family; who it was I do not know, but he was young and handsome and cut a fine figure. He must have been something on the order of Middle Captain of the Inner Palace Guards.

This man was making a secret pilgrimage to Kiyomizu[1] when he saw a very pretty woman, gracefully and handsomely dressed, walking toward him. She was of good birth, he could see; and she was evidently making a secret pilgrimage on foot. She glanced up at him unconcernedly and he observed that she was twenty or a little older. Her face was so lovely, so beguiling, that in all the world there could be none like her. "Whoever can she be?" he wondered. And how could he not pay her his addresses? Such passion was aroused in him that he forgot everything but courting her. Seeing her emerge from the central hall of the temple, he summoned a page boy and said to him, "Follow her and find out where her home is."

After the captain had returned home, the page boy came to him. "I kept a sharp lookout," he said. "Her house is not in the capital at all but south of Kiyomizu, north of Amida's Peak.[2] The house looks awfully grand. There was an older lady with her, and when she saw me following them she said, 'What are you up to, boy? You seem to be giving us the honor of your company.' 'My master saw your mistress at the temple in Kiyomizu and ordered me to find out where her home is,' I said. And then, just imagine, she said, 'If you come this way again, pay us a visit.' " The captain was delighted with the boy's report and sent a letter, and the lady replied in an exquisite hand.

The captain and the boy hasten from the house of the robber.

And thus letters went back and forth. In one of her replies the
lady said, "A rustic like me cannot make visits to the capital — but
won't you come here? I should like to speak with you, though of
course there will be a screen between us." The captain was wildly
impatient to see her; overjoyed, he set out on horseback, accompanied only by two attendants, the page boy, and a groom. He left
the capital just as it was dark to avoid being noticed.

Upon arriving, he sent the page ahead to announce him. The
older woman came out and said "This way, sirs," and they followed her into the compound. The mud and timber wall encir-
cling it was very stout, and the gates were high, and there was a
dry moat in the garden with a bridge across it. The captain left his
horse and companions at a building outside the moat and crossed
the bridge alone. Beyond it were a great many buildings. There
was one which he decided must be the apartment for receiving
guests. He went through an outer door[3] and looked around him.
Careful arrangements had been made for his reception. Folding
screens and curtains of state had been set up, handsome mats
spread out,[4] and blinds hung about the central chamber.

Rustic it might be, thought the captain, but this was obviously
the home of a lady of fashion! The furnishings bespoke her refinement, he thought. It was far into the night when the lady
herself appeared. Without further ado, he went inside her curtains of state, and they lay down together. They became intimate.
Afterwards he found her even more beautiful than when he had
first glimpsed her.

As they lay there the captain told her how he had longed for
her these many days past, and he vowed that he would love her
forever, but the woman looked anxious and preoccupied, and it
seemed to him that she was secretly crying. The captain thought
this strange. "What's the matter?" he asked. "You seem unhappy
over something."

"It's only a mood," she said. "There's no cause for it." The
captain thought this even stranger.

"Now that we are so well acquainted you must hide nothing
from me. What is it?" he said. "I can see that something is
wrong." He questioned her insistently.

"I don't want to hide it; it's only that it's so painful to speak of,"
she said through her tears.

"Tell me straight out," the captain said. "Whatever it may be, even — even if it is that I must die!"

"Indeed," said the woman, "I must not hide it from you. I am the daughter of a certain person in the capital" — and she named him — "but my parents both died and I was left an orphan. The master of this house is a beggar who has become enormously wealthy. He has lived in this place and in this manner for many years. By his contrivance I was kidnapped and brought here to be his ward. He outfits me in fine style. Every so often he has me visit Kiyomizu. Men who see me make advances to me, as you did, and they are lured here, as you were. While they sleep a spear is thrust down from the ceiling. I guide it to the man's chest, and he is stabbed to death. His corpse is stripped, and the companions he has left in the building outside the moat are all murdered, and they are stripped and their mounts are taken. Twice already it has happened, and it will go on and on. That will be my life! But this time I have decided to point the spear at myself and die in your stead. Make haste to escape! The people who were with you will all be dead by now. I grieve only because I will never see you again." And she wept unrestrainedly.

When the captain heard this his senses all but failed him, but he forced himself to think, and he said, "This is horrible! And that you should offer to die for me — No, no! I am grateful, but I can't save myself and abandon you. Let us escape together."

"I have thought it over again and again," the woman said, "and if the spear does not strike flesh, my master will hurry down to see what is the matter. If we are gone he will give chase, and then we will surely both be killed. Save your own life, my lord, and after I am dead perform holy works and dedicate them to my soul. How could I go on committing such crimes!"

"No holy work can repay the sacrifice of your life for mine," said the captain. "But since that is your wish, I shall try to escape."

The woman said, "The bridge across the moat must have been pulled up as soon as you crossed, but if you go out the sliding door over there you can make your way along a narrow bank on the other side of the moat. The outer wall has a small opening where water is let in, and if you are careful, you can just crawl through. The time has come. When the spear is lowered I will hold it to my breast, be impaled, and die." Even as she spoke, voices were heard from within the house, a sound terrible beyond the power of words to describe.

The captain arose even as he was weeping and tucked up the hem of the single gown he wore. He stole out the sliding door as he had been told, made his way along the bank, and just managed to crawl through the hole in the wall. So far so good; but now he had no idea which way to go and simply ran straight ahead. Footsteps sounded behind him. "They've come after me," he thought. He looked back in helpless terror and saw that it was his young page boy. "How did you do it?" he asked, overjoyed.

The boy said, "The moment you crossed the moat, they pulled up the bridge. I thought there was something funny going on, so I sneaked back over the wall. I heard the others being killed. 'What has become of my master?' I wondered miserably. I couldn't go back home, so I hid in the bushes to watch and listen. Then I heard someone running. 'Could it be —?' I thought, and I came after you."

"A horrible business," said the captain. "I had no notion of the true state of affairs." Together they ran toward the capital. Near the place where Fifth Avenue crosses the Kamo River they turned to look back and saw great flames rising from the direction in which the house had been.

The beggar assumed that the man had been stabbed; but when he did not hear the woman's voice as usual he became suspicious and hurried down. The man was gone and the woman lay dead. If the man succeeded in escaping, he himself would immediately be arrested, he realized, and without further ado he set fire to all the buildings and fled.

Once home, the captain swore the page to silence, and he himself never mentioned the incident to anyone. Every year, however, he had Buddhist rites celebrated on a grand scale without saying on whose behalf they were. But actually, it seems, the merit from that holy work was dedicated to the woman's soul. The story got out, and someone built a temple on the ruins of the house where she had lived. [I can't recall its name].[5] It still exists today.

Now think: the woman was truly of noble mind, and what's more, the boy was loyal and astute. But people who've heard this story take it as a warning: don't just wander off as you please to an unfamiliar place at the sight of some lovely woman. So the tale's been told, and so it's been handed down.

Notes to Story 28

1. The Kiyomizu temple, in the Higashiyama area of present-day Kyoto, east of the original boundaries of the capital.

2. Also in Higashiyama-ku, on the road from Kyoto to Yamashina.

3. *Tsumado,* large double-leaved hinged doors at the four corners of the principal buildings within a Heian domestic compound, the chief means of access into the interior chamber.

4. Mats at this time did not cover the entire flooring, were comparatively thin, and were used as cushions later came to be used.

5. Bridging a lacuna in the original; literally "called the —— temple, it still exists today."

5. HOW A POOR MAN LEFT HIS WIFE AND HOW SHE BECAME THE WIFE OF THE GOVERNOR OF SETTSU

AT A TIME NOW PAST, there was in the capital a man of no special standing. He had no friends and neither parents nor relations, and having nowhere of his own to lodge, he went to others for employment. But since none of his masters paid him the attention he thought he deserved, he went from place to place, always in hope of something better. Everywhere, though, it was the same. He was unfit to serve a noble family, and he had no way of earning a living. His wife was young and good-looking, a woman of refined temperament who clung loyally to her impoverished husband. In the depths of his anxiety he told her: "I thought that we would spend our whole lives together, but with every passing day I become poorer. I wonder if our marriage is not the cause of my misfortune. How would it be if we were to go our separate ways?" His wife disagreed. "Good and ill fortune comes from the karma of our previous lives. I was willing to starve with you if need be. But it is hopeless to go on in this way, and if you really think our marriage might be the cause, let us try separating." This was what the man wanted, and amidst tears and vows of eternal love, they parted.

Afterwards the wife, being young and good-looking, found employment at the house of a man [whose name is no longer known]. Since she was a woman of refinement, he used her with great kindness, and when his wife died he called her to serve him intimately. He had her sleep by his side and became fond of her. As time passed he came to treat this mistress as his wife and entrusted all his household affairs to her.

Meanwhile this man became governor of Settsu.[1] The woman passed her years in ever increasing prosperity. Her original husband had thought his luck might improve if he were separated from her, but instead he fell on even harder times. In the end he was unable to remain in the capital and in the course of his wanderings went to Settsu Province. He became a mere farmhand whom others hired, doing peasants' work, tilling fields and cutting wood. But he couldn't get used to the idea, couldn't do the work at all. His employer sent him to the bay of Naniwa[2] to cut reeds. He went to Naniwa to cut reeds — and the governor and his wife went to Settsu Province. By Naniwa Bay they halted their carriage to enjoy the view. With their numerous retainers and followers they ate and drank and amused themselves. The wife sat in the carriage with her ladies, admiring the view and the interesting and charming spectacles it offered. There were a great many people of the lowest class cutting reeds; and among them one who, though of the same class, seemed somehow to be of finer stuff.

The governor's wife saw him and stared: how strangely like her former husband he was! Perhaps she was mistaken, she thought, and looked harder; but it was indeed he. He made a strange figure, standing there cutting reeds. What a pitiful wretch he was! she thought. Surely he must be suffering for the sins of a previous life. Tears welled up, but pretending that nothing was amiss, she summoned a servant. "There's a certain man among the reed-cutters," she said, describing him. "Call him over." The messenger ran. "You there — over to their honors' carriage," he said. It was so unexpected that the man just gaped at him in astonishment. "Hurry up!" the messenger shouted. Scared, the man dropped the reeds he had cut, thrust his scythe into his belt, and went up to the carriage.

Observing him from close by, she knew that it truly was he. He wore a hemp shirt, black with filth and without sleeves, that scarcely reached his knees. A soiled cloth covered his head. Earth clung to his face, to his hands and feet: he was utterly filthy. Leeches were sucking at the backs of his knees and his shanks, exposing the raw flesh. The governor's lady saw him with pity and revulsion, and she had one of her people give him food and saké. She examined his face as he squatted in front of her carriage eating and found it repellent. To her maids she said, "This man seems of a better class than the other reed-cutters. I feel sorry for him," and she had someone take a robe from within the carriage, with instructions to give it to him. On a scrap of paper that accompanied the robe, she wrote:

>*"I'll be fortunate,"*[3]
>*You thought,*
>*And so we parted—*
>*Why then, why then*
>*Do you live by Naniwa Bay?*

The man received the robe. The gift was entirely unexpected. Looking at it in wonderment, he saw a scrap of paper with something written on it; and when he took that and saw what was written, he thought: "Why, this is my former wife!" How sad and shameful was his destiny, he now realized. "Give me your ink-stone," he said. She gave it to him, and this is what he wrote:

>*Without you*
>*I'm unfortunate indeed,*
>*I know;*
>*How hard it is, how hard it is*
>*To live by Naniwa Bay.*

When the governor's lady saw this she pitied him even more. The man cut no more reeds but ran away and hid. Afterwards the lady never spoke of this to anyone.

Everything is reward or retribution for the deeds of our previous lives; it is ignorance that makes a man resent his fate.

The story must have been told by the governor's lady in her old age. So the tale goes, and so it will be handed down for generations to come.

Notes to Story 5

1. See 29:18, note 1.

2. Naniwa was the ancient name for modern Osaka.

3. There are untranslatable puns in this poem and the text, sources of their wit and, in part, of their pathos. *Ashikaraji,* "I'll be fortunate" (more literally, "it will not be ill-omened") also means "I'll not cut reeds"; *ashikaru,* "I'm unfortunate indeed" (literally, "it is ill-omened") also means "I cut reeds."

Chapter Thirty-One

7. HOW THE MINOR CONTROLLER OF THE RIGHT MOROIE NO ASON ENCOUNTERED A WOMAN AND DIED

AT A TIME NOT LONG PAST, there was a man named Fujiwara no Moroie[1] who was Minor Controller of the Right. He had a mistress who loved him as he loved her and whom he visited regularly. This woman was of a very gentle and yielding disposition, and when she had a grievance she kept it in her heart unspoken. All too often, the Controller unintentionally did something to hurt her. He might be occupied with public business; or on impulse he might spend the night with a prostitute. He let more and more time elapse between his visits, and the woman, who was unaccustomed to neglect, became resentful. But all the while she never let her feelings show, and meanwhile his visits became rare. Things between them were no longer as they had been. She was not *exactly* angry with him — and yet she was resentful. As time went on she became more and more dissatisfied, so that in the end, with no actual quarrel between them, the relationship was broken off.

It was perhaps half a year later that the Controller passed by the house just as a servant was coming in from an errand. "Fancy who's passing by! It's none other than his lordship the Controller. When was it that he used to visit here? What a pity that we never see him any more!" The mistress of the house heard this and sent someone out with a message. Would he step inside for a moment? She had something to tell him. With this, the Controller suddenly realized where he was. He got down from his carriage, sent it back home, and went into the house. The woman was facing a sutra box. She wore supple robes and exquisite trousers of fine raw silk. It was evident that hers was no hastily repaired toilette but that she had been sitting there composedly, handsomely arrayed. The expression in her eyes and about her forehead was utterly charming. The Controller felt as though he were seeing her for the first time. "Why have I never looked at her until

now?" he asked himself over and over again. If only he could get
the sutra away from her, stop her from reading it, go to bed with
her! But they had been apart for months, and he felt compunc-
tions about forcing himself upon her. He tried to start a conversation, but she did not answer. When the sutra reading was over,
then they would talk, her face seemed to say—and how beautiful
it was! If there was any way to restore their past relationship it
must be restored, he thought wildly; and he remained there. "If
ever after I should be tempted to neglect her"—in his heart he
made ten thousand vows. Repeatedly he told her how little it had
meant that he had been remiss these many months; but she did
not answer. She reached the seventh scroll and repeated the King
of Medicine chapter; three times over she read it.

"What do you think you're doing?" said the Controller.
"Hurry and be done with your reading! I have a great deal to say
to you." Just then she was reading the passage which goes:

> "When her life is ended she will
>   forthwith be reborn in paradise;
> There where lives Amida Buddha
>   surrounded by his holy throng
> She will sit upon a jeweled throne
>   within a blue lotus."[2]

Tears welled from her eyes. "Enough of this nonsense!" said
the Controller. "Have you become pious? You put on the airs of a
nun." He met her brimming gaze, and it was as though dew had
drenched the frost. He had a foreboding of misfortune: how hard-
hearted she must have thought him all these months! He too
could not restrain his tears. How would he feel if he were never to
see her again, he mused with a sinking heart, and he was filled
with bitter remorse.

But no sooner had the woman finished reading the sutra than
she began manipulating a rosary inlaid with amber. She was deep
in concentration: and then she paused and raised her eyes. Suddenly her expression altered strangely. "What's this?" he
thought. "I called you in because I wanted to see you face to face
once more. And now my anger—" she said, and died. The Controller was aghast. "Someone come!" he shouted, but at first no
one paid any attention. After a time someone did hear, and a
senior maid stuck her head in. "Is anything wrong?" she said. The

Controller sat there dumbfounded. "How strange! What on earth can have happened!" she said — and was there not good reason for her consternation?

Nothing could be done. The woman had died, and that was that. It had taken no more time than it takes a hair to snap. For all that he felt, the Controller could not remain in a house where there was a defilement, and so he returned home. In his sorrow the vision of her face as it had once been floated before his eyes. But even so: how was he to have known?

Not long after his return, the Controller himself took sick; and not many days later he died. It must have been that he was possessed by the woman's spirit. He and those close to him must have known that it was the woman's spirit.

There are people whose view is that since the woman spent her last moments reading the Lotus Sutra she was assured of rebirth in paradise; but then one remembers that she died overcome with rancor upon seeing the Controller. How deep was the sinfulness of both! So the tale's been told, and so it's been handed down.

Notes to Story 7

1. Moroie died in 1058, not long after being appointed to the lower fourth rank junior grade. He was in his thirty-second year at the time (according to some commentators, his fortieth).

2. For a more literal, authoritative translation of this passage, see Leon Hurvitz, *Scripture of the Lotus Blossom of the Fine Dharma* (New York: Columbia, 1976), p. 300. The passage enumerates the benefits of hearing and practicing this chapter of the Lotus Sutra. The woman who hears it will be reborn as a man; reborn in paradise; freed of anger, folly, envy, and other defilements of passion.

31. ABOUT THE OLD WOMAN WHO SOLD FISH AT THE HEADQUARTERS OF THE CROWN PRINCE'S GUARD

AT A TIME NOW PAST, when the former Emperor Sanjō was crown prince,[1] there was a woman who came regularly to the headquarters of the Crown Prince's Guard[2] to sell fish. The officers of the guard sent someone to buy some, and tasted it. It had a delicious flavor, and so they made it a staple of their meals, the favorite accompaniment for their rice. The fish had been dried and was in tiny slices.

Now, in the eighth month of the year the guards were in Kitano enjoying some hawking[3] when they came across the woman. The guards recognized her face. What on earth could a low creature like that be doing here, they wondered, and galloped over to her. She was carrying a capacious-looking bamboo tub, and she held a whip upraised. At the sight of the guards she cowered as though she would flee; she was quaking from head to foot. The guards' attendants approached her and tried to see what was in the tub, but she clutched it to her and refused to show it to them. Their suspicions aroused, they snatched it away. Inside they saw snakes cut into four-inch lengths. "What's this for?" they asked, but she did not answer and just stood there trembling. It turned out that what the villainous creature did was frighten snakes from the thickets with a whip and kill them when they crawled out; then she would cut them up and carry them home, cure them with salt, dry them, and sell them. And that is what the guards, all unknowing, had made a staple of their meals.

Now think: it's said that eating snakes makes people sick. You wonder why they weren't poisoned.

Everyone who's heard this story agrees that you must have your wits about you when you buy fish to eat. Don't buy it if it's been cut so fine that you can't tell what it looked like originally. So the tale's been told, and so it's been handed down.

Notes to Story 31

1. Between 986, when he was made crown prince, and 1011, when he was enthroned.

2. *Tachihaki,* a group of official retainers *(toneri)* assigned as bodyguard to the crown prince.

3. There was an autumn hawking season, for small birds, called *kotagari;* the principal hawking season was in winter. Kitano was an open area north of the imperial enclosure.

37. ABOUT THE GREAT OAK
IN KURUMOTO DISTRICT
IN ŌMI PROVINCE

AT A TIME NOW PAST, in Kurumoto District in Ōmi Province,[1] there grew a great oak tree. It was five hundred arm-spans around, so you can imagine how high it was and how thick its branches. Its shade fell as far as Tanba Province in the morning and Ise Province in the evening. In thunderstorms it did not move; typhoons might blow, but it did not shake.

But the folk of three districts of that province, Shiga, Kurumoto, and Kōga, were unable to grow crops, for the tree's shade so covered the fields that the sun's light never struck them. On this account the folk of the several districts petitioned the Emperor. The Emperor thereupon despatched Kanimori no Sukune,[2] along with others, and they cut the tree down in accordance with the farmers' request. And after that tree was cut down, the farmers obtained rich harvests from their fields.

The descendants of the farmers who complained to the Emperor live in those districts even today.

A queer tale, isn't it! So the tale's been told, and so it's been handed down.

Notes to Story 37

1. Southeast of Lake Biwa, in modern Shiga prefecture.

2. Not identifiable. *Kanimori* implies that the person was a member of the imperial household's Bureau of Housekeeping, and *Sukune* is a hereditary clan title.